EXPLORING THE STORY

THE STORY PRODUCT LINE

The Story Church Campaign Kit
Bible Engagement for Adults, Teens, and Children

There's a new story unfolding. People in churches and in homes everywhere are experiencing God's Word in a whole new way. *The Story Church Campaign Kit* provides all tools you need to draw your congregation, your small group, and your family into the grand, unfolding story of the Bible as one sweeping narrative, arranged chronologically from Genesis to Revelation.

Church Campaign Kit   9780310941538   **$149.99**

THE STORY FOR ADULTS

The Story, NIV
The Bible as One Continuing Story of God and His People

Hardcover   9780310950974 $19.99
CASE QUANTITY PRICING AVAILABLE

The Story Curriculum DVD
Getting to the Heart of God's Story

DVD   025986329525 $29.99

The Story Curriculum Participant's Guide
Getting to the Heart of God's Story

Softcover   9780310329534 $10.99
CASE QUANTITY PRICING AVAILABLE

The Story, NIV Audio CD
The Bible as One Continuing Story of God and His People

Audio CD, Unabridged
   025986421779 $34.99

THE STORY FOR YOUTH

The Story: Teen Edition, NIV
Read the Bible as One Seamless Story from Beginning to End

Softcover   9780310722809   **$14.99**
CASE QUANTITY PRICING AVAILABLE

The Story: Teen Curriculum
Finding Your Place in the Story of God

DVD   025986413712   **$49.99**

The Story for Kids, NIRV
Discover the Bible from Beginning to End

Softcover   9780310719250   **$9.99**
CASE QUANTITY PRICING AVAILABLE

The Story: Elementary Curriculum
31 Lessons

CD-ROM   9780310719229   **$34.99**

The Story for Children, a Storybook Bible

Hardcover   9780310719755   **$19.99**
CASE QUANTITY PRICING AVAILABLE

The Story: Early Elementary Curriculum   31 Lessons

CD-ROM   9780310719212   **$34.99**

The Story for Little Ones
Discover the Bible in Pictures

Hardcover   9780310719274   **$17.99**

The Story: Preschool Curriculum
31 Lessons

CD-ROM   9780310719205   **$34.99**

EXPLORING THE STORY

A REFERENCE COMPANION

ADAM T. BARR

ZONDERVAN

Exploring the Story
Copyright © 2011 by Zondervan

This title is also available as a Zondervan ebook.
Visit www.zondervan.com/ebooks.

Requests for information should be addressed to:

Zondervan, 3900 *Sparks Dr. SE, Grand Rapids, Michigan* 49546

Library of Congress Cataloging-in-Publication Data

Barr, Adam T.
    Exploring the Story : a reference companion / Adam T. Barr.
       p. cm.
    ISBN 978-0-310-32699-1 (softcover)
    1. Bible—Textbooks. 2. Bible—Chronology. I. Title.
  BS605.3.B38 2011
  220.6'1—dc22
                            2010034992

Interior design: Beth Shagene

Printed in the United States of America

14 15 16 17 18 19 20 /DCI/ 27 26 25 24 23 22 21 20 19 18 17 16 15 14 13 12 11 10

For my wife, Jen,
because your faithful prayers accomplish much

CONTENTS

PREFACE

This reference guide serves as a companion to *The Story*, which captures the biblical story line in thirty-one chapters. If you are a preaching pastor, teacher, student ministries leader, or someone who just wants to go deeper in biblical study, this guide will help you do that. Each chapter in this reference guide corresponds to a chapter in *The Story* and provides helpful background information as you prepare sermons, craft lessons, or simply take time to expand your understanding of Scripture. Every chapter is broken into the following sections:

- *Timeline.* Get a sense of the "big picture." How do the events in *The Story* relate to the rest of history? Every chapter contains a helpful timeline that coordinates biblical and secular events.
- *Plot Points.* These short lists cut to the heart of each chapter and reveal the key themes.
- *Cast of Characters.* This list of every character in each chapter will help you get a sense of "who fits where." In addition to a name, you will find a brief description and, if available, the meaning of that person's name.
- *Chapter Overview.* A brief two to three paragraph summary of each chapter.
- *Section Commentary.* Each chapter in *The Story* covers some major events. We break down these events and provide commentary. Each section commentary provides deeper insight into theological issues, relevant archaeological discoveries, or just a powerful launch point for further reflection.
- *Discussion Questions. The Story* has a set of discussion questions in the back. We have crafted more questions for individual reflection or group study.

In addition to these chapters, I would refer you to the appendix. There you will find a brief annotated bibliography that will help you expand your investigation. I pray you will find your journey through *The Story* as exciting as I did!

God Bless,
ADAM T. BARR

CREATION
The Beginning of Life as We Know It

1

Plot Points

- God, the main character of *The Story*, is revealed as the absolute sovereign of creation, totally distinct from yet intimately involved with all he has made.
- Nature is not simply a collection of random, meaningless matter in motion; it is a carefully crafted revelation of a loving God.
- Humanity, made in God's image, occupies a unique role and position in this creation, a place of dignity and responsibility.
- Humanity's tragic rebellion against God's command impacts *everything*.
- God has a plan to redeem his fallen creation, giving us a hint of the good news to come in his promise that a descendant of Adam and Eve will crush the serpent.
- Throughout the New Testament, the flood story forecasts God's future and final judgment (e.g., Matt. 24:37 – 39; Luke 17:26 – 27; 2 Peter 2:4 – 10).

The Days of Creation

Day 1	Light and dark	Days of forming
Day 2	Sky and water	
Day 3	Land	
Day 4	Sun, moon, and stars	Days of filling
Day 5	Birds and sea creatures	
Day 6	Animals and humans	
Day 7	God's Sabbath	Day of rest

Cast of Characters

Abel. Son of Adam and Eve; younger brother of Cain; a shepherd and devoted worshiper of the Lord; killed by his brother; name means "vanity, breath, vapor."

Adam. First man, made from earth; husband of Eve; like his wife, Eve, made in God's image; tragically disobeyed God's prohibition and affected all of human history; name can mean "man" and is closely related to the Hebrew word for "ground" (*adamah*).

Cain. Son of Adam and Eve; older brother and murderer of Abel; ancestor of Lamech, who killed indiscriminately (see Gen. 4:23 – 24); name sounds like the Hebrew for "gotten,"

God measures the earth he has created in this illustration from a mid-thirteenth-century Bible.

Eric Lessing/Art Resource, NY

conveying the sense of optimism Eve held for his life.

Eve. First woman, made from man; wife of Adam; tempted by Satan in the form of a serpent, disobeyed God's command; name means "living."

God. Creator of all things and central character of *The Story*; God chose to reveal himself to us through his creation.

Noah. Descendant of Adam and Eve; a "righteous man, blameless among the people of his time" (Gen. 6:9); commanded to build a great boat to save himself and his family from the flood God sent to wipe out everything having "the breath of life" (Gen. 6:17); name sounds like "rest" in Hebrew, expressing his parents' hope that he would help bring rest from the effects of the curse.

Shem, Ham, Japheth. Noah's three sons; called to help "increase in number and fill the earth" (Gen. 9:1) after the flood.

Chapter Overview

The first nine chapters of Genesis have raised questions throughout church history. What kind of literature are these passages? How do the events described here relate to the theories formed by contemporary scientists and archaeologists? Are the "days" twenty-four-hour segments or *ages*, long periods of time? Was the flood local, covering the known world, or was it global, covering the entire planet?

These questions are significant. They lead us to think deeply about the purpose of Scripture, and Christians who take Scripture as seriously as Jesus did will not be content simply to write these questions off as "academic." To work toward the answers we seek, it is helpful to begin by reflecting on the central narrative intent of these chapters. For the people of Israel and for us today, they reveal *why* the world we see and know is the way it is. They help us grasp what it means to be human and the causal forces that shape our lives. These are questions of existence and meaning.

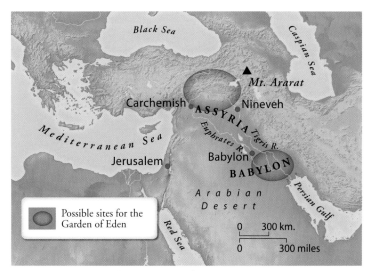

Possible locations of the garden of Eden.

Think about the fall and the disobedience of Adam and Eve in Genesis 3. The fruit of their rebellion against God is a series of curses, each of which takes a good, God-ordained source of blessing and twists it into a form of heartache — work is now toil, marriage a battle, childbirth a painful ordeal. Consider the flood as well. In this story we see a reversal of God's work in creation as the life and the land that had come from the sea is now covered and destroyed by the waters of chaos and judgment. The stunning beauty and heart-wrenching tragedy of our world is explained and understood through these stories, helping us understand why something good has gone terribly wrong.

God's Word invites us to consider the powerful connections between the original world God created, our disobedience, and our ongoing relationship to God. We are invited to consider how human disobedience has universal implications. Although we often think of our choices as individual decisions that don't impact other people ("If it doesn't hurt anyone else, it's not a problem"), this chapter shows us that the simple act of eating fruit, if done in disobedience to God, can lead to suffering and death — for everyone. The choices and decisions we make

in this life are writing a moral drama, and our every deed illustrates how we embrace or reject our Creator God.

One more thing: consider how this chapter reveals *God* as the supreme storyteller. Unlike a human author who relies on words and print to convey a story, God is enacting a grand narrative in flesh and blood, neutrons and nebulae. Throughout the course of your study, remember who the central character is and what he is saying in this story.

Section Commentary

The Creation of All Things
(Genesis 1 – 2)

Just as the Creation story stood against the polytheistic myths of the ancient Near East, today it provides us with an alternative to the materialistic myth of evolution. Much of the current debate between proponents of creation and evolution can be simplified to one question: *Where do we come from?* If human life is ultimately the product of an unguided, cause-

A Phoenician ivory from the 9th-8th century B.C. depicts two figures worshiping the tree of life.

Z. Radovan/www.BibleLandPictures.com

and-effect chain reaction stretching back to the Big Bang, then concepts like human rights and moral norms are just code words for majority opinion. If, however, we let the Creation story set the stage of our existence, then we are the product of a powerful, creative God. We are not here by accident, and we ultimately are accountable to the God who put us here. He stands as the ultimate arbiter of right and wrong, not us. These worldviews present us with two contrast-ing answers to the question of our origin and lead to two very different ways to live.

The Tragic Fall (Genesis 3–4)

"What is wrong with the world?" Everyone is trying to answer this question, whether he or she realizes it or not. At some level we all sense that something big is broken. Cosmic scales are waiting to be balanced. We understand what it feels like as we constantly try to change some-thing about ourselves but find that we fail every time. What is wrong with the world? And what is wrong with us? Why are things so "out of joint"?

The story of Genesis 3–4 answers those questions. We read that things are the way they are because humans, at the very beginning, chose to live life on their own terms. Human-kind chose independence and rebellion rather than trust and obedience.

Humans constantly try to come to grips with the world we inhabit. On the one hand, we sense that much about this world is good. People are capable of amazing heroism and selfless sacrifice. On the other hand, unspeak-able tragedy occurs and horrific evils are com-mitted every day all over the world. The story of the fall tells us why things are this way. The goodness of God's creation could not be wholly destroyed by our sin and rebellion, but until the story is over, we cannot experience the good life God intended apart from the taint of sin and the curse. We live in a fallen world, waiting to be redeemed and made new by the Creator.

The Great Flood (Genesis 6–9)

In the creation story, we saw the Lord sepa-rating light from darkness, the waters below from the waters above, and the land from the water. In each case God was refining his creation and crafting the perfect environment for creatures. After setting the stage, God began filling it with life!

In the flood, however, we see a reversal of this process. The heavens rain down. The earth is covered in the waters of chaos. A world teeming with life becomes a global graveyard. Everything with "the breath of life in its nostrils" is destroyed (Gen. 7:22). Later in Scripture the apostle Paul will write that the "wages of sin is death" (Rom. 6:23). In this passage we discover just how true that really is.

The ancient Near East abounded with creation stories, but not one revealed the Creator God of Genesis 1 and 2. For instance, the Babylonian Genesis told of the goddess Tiamat, who gave birth to all the gods. Eventually, she was killed by her son Marduk. Her dead corpse became the earth. Human beings were created to take care of the world so the gods could relax.

Discussion Questions

1. What words would you use to describe the God who is revealed in the Creation narrative?

2. The story of the fall indicates that every part of God's good creation was fractured by Adam and Eve's rebellion. As you observe our world, what evidence do you see that the world was created to be a good and beautiful place? Where do you see evidence that it is broken by sin?

3. In the flood story, we encounter a God who takes action to prevent the spread of human rebellion and sin by destroying most of his creation. The flood is both an act of judgment and salvation. How do you see these two activities of God reflected in the story? How do these themes differ from the "popular" picture of God that is often presented in this passage?

2

GOD BUILDS A NATION

Plot Points

- God calls Abraham out of the darkness of pagan idolatry into the light of true fellowship.
- God works through a covenant, making Abraham and his descendants his chosen people, marking out a special land for their inheritance, and promising to bless all nations through Abraham's family.
- When Abraham and Sarah try to make God's plan work through their own efforts, things get very messy.
- God keeps his promise, miraculously giving Abraham and Sarah a son in their old age; one generation later Jacob will produce twelve sons of his own and the nation of Israel will be born.

The Chosen Family (2200–1800 B.C.)

Biblical	Secular
2166 Abraham born 2091 Abraham moves to Canaan 2066 Sarah gives birth to Isaac 2050 Abraham offers Isaac 2006 Rebekah gives birth to Jacob and Esau 1991 Abraham dies 1915 Rachel gives birth to Joseph	2160–2010 The First Intermediate Period (Egypt), marked by regional famine and a general decline in Egyptian culture. 2112–2095 King Ur-Nammu restores the Sumerian kingdom and develops a law code and justice system. He dies "abandoned on the field of battle like a broken pot." But his son Shulgi (2094–2047) ushered in a period of peace. 2106–1786 The Middle Kingdom, a period of renaissance and growth in Egypt. 2000 Epic of Gilgamesh records the Sumerian flood legend.

Cast of Characters

Abram. Husband of Sarah, father of Isaac and Ishmael; called the "father of faith" for his steadfast trust in God's promise to make him the "father of many nations"; God changed his name from Abram ("exalted father") to Abraham ("father of a multitude").

Benjamin. Son of Jacob and Rachel; his mother died giving birth to him and named him Ben-oni, "son of my sorrow" or "son of my strength"; renamed Benjamin by his father, meaning "son of the right hand."

Eliezer. From Damascus; a trusted part of Abraham's household, perhaps a slave; name means "God is help."

Esau. Firstborn son of Isaac and Rebekah; a hunter and man of action; swindled out of his inheritance by his younger brother and his own shortsightedness; name means "red."

Hagar. Sarah's Egyptian servant; given to Abraham as a wife to produce offspring; mother of Ishmael; experienced God's favor; name means "stranger or one who fears."

Isaac. The child promised to Abraham and Sarah; father of Jacob, called "Israel"; name means "he laughs."

Ishmael. Abraham's son by Hagar; while not the child of promise, given a great blessing by God; name means "God hears."

Jacob. Second-born son of Isaac and Rebekah; received the promised blessing and inheritance of a firstborn son; married to Leah and Rachel; father of twelve sons who became the twelve tribes of Israel; name means "he takes by the heel" or "he cheats"; name changed to Israel ("strives with God") after a wrestling match with God.

Leah. Daughter of Laban; Jacob's first and least-loved wife; she was the mother of Issachar, Zebulun, Simeon, Levi, Judah, and Reuben; her servant, Zilpah, produced two more sons for her, Gad and Asher; name means "weary, tired."

Lot. Son of Haran; nephew of Abraham; rescued by Abraham after being kidnapped; rescued again by two angels from the destruction of Sodom and Gomorrah; name means "wrapped up, hidden."

Melchizedek. A priest and king in Jerusalem who prefigured Jesus Christ; graciously provided food and drink for Abraham and his servant, receiving a tithe in return; name means "king of righteousness."

Rachel. Daughter of Laban; Jacob's true love; the mother of Joseph and Benjamin; servant, Bilhah, produced two more sons for her, Dan and Naphtali; name means "sheep."

Rebekah. A distant relative of Abraham; daughter of Bethuel; sister to Laban; married Isaac and had two sons, Jacob and Esau; given a prophetic word for her two sons, that the older would serve the younger; name means "fat, fattened."

Reuben. Jacob and Leah's son; violated Jacob's concubine, a decision he would later regret; name means "see, a son."

Sarai. Wife of Abram; miraculously gave birth to Isaac in her advanced years; a beautiful woman and, according to Peter, a model of godly womanhood (1 Peter 3:1–6); both *Sarai*, her original name, and *Sarah*, the name given her by God, mean "princess."

Chapter Overview

One of the first things we notice about the unfolding story of Scripture is that God is the central character driving the action and moving the plot forward: he does not need us to accomplish his purposes. We are characters in his story, not the other way around. Contrary to popular caricatures of God, he is not sitting around in heaven, wringing his hands in powerless frustration. Far from it!

In fact, God often chooses to accomplish his purposes in the most difficult way possible. Although we may scratch our heads and

The Epic of Gilgamesh includes a clay tablet that describes a big flood that occurred around the fifteenth century B.C.

wonder why God chooses to work in this way, the reason soon becomes quite clear: God is reminding us that he is the one in charge, and *nothing* will frustrate his purposes. The story

of Abraham (originally Abram) is a perfect case in point. God determines to build a great nation, give them a promised land, and bless all nations through them. He wants to reveal himself to them, entrust them with his Word, and bring his own Son to earth through them. So who does he choose to found this great nation? None other than a man and woman well past the normal childbearing age. God's ways are certainly not our ways!

We learn something fundamental about God in his curious choice of Abraham: it is God's grace, not our own effort, that matters most in the story. And this is something we should pay careful attention to, because it is not the last time we will encounter this theme as the story unfolds.

Section Commentary

Abraham Called into God's Promise (Genesis 12–13, 15; Romans 4; Hebrews 11)

Joshua 24:2–3 tells us that Abraham was part of a pagan family:

> Joshua said to all the people, "This is what the LORD, the God of Israel, says: 'Long ago your forefathers, including Terah the father of Abraham and Nahor, lived beyond the Euphrates River and worshiped other gods. But I took your father Abraham from the land beyond the Euphrates and led him throughout Canaan and gave him many descendants.

The ancient Near East was a place with many gods, each one believed to meet a specific need and to demand specific sacrifices. For Abraham to look to just one God to supply all his needs was radically counterculture in his day.

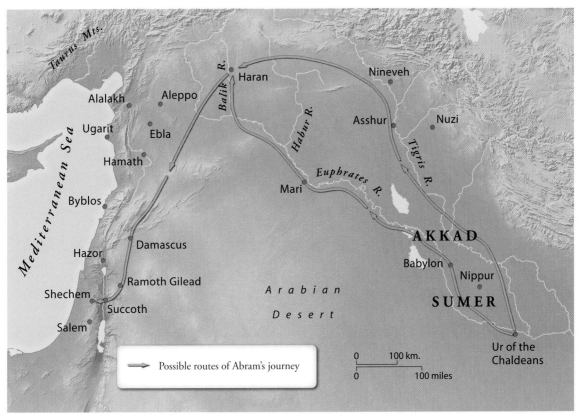

Abram's travels.

Abraham Takes Things into His Own Hands (Genesis 16)

The ancient world placed an enormous importance on producing offspring to safeguard the family inheritance. Marriage contracts would even outline potential options in case of infertility. Husbands could divorce infertile wives, take on concubines, practice polygyny (multiple wives of equal status), or adopt an heir if their first wife did not produce one. Sarah's suggestion might offend our modern sensibilities, but it was the norm in her day. Still, in light of God's promise, it revealed her lack of faith in God's promise and reminds us

that when God's people look to the surrounding culture for their values, we take our eyes off of what God values.

The Covenant of Circumcision (Genesis 17)

Circumcision was a common practice in the ancient world and was not unique to the descendants of Abraham. In Egypt it was an adolescent rite of passage, and it was regularly practiced in Canaanite culture as well. What made the mark of circumcision unique for Abraham was the God who demanded it. As this passage reveals, the mark of circumcision was intended to serve

These clay figurines from the 10th–7th centuries B.C. were worshiped as house deities. Asherah was the Canaanite goddess of fertility.

as a constant physical reminder that Abraham and his descendants had been called out and blessed so that they could be a blessing to their neighbors. In the covenant God not only promised blessing for his people, but he demanded faithful obedience.

The Promise Fulfilled (Genesis 21)

One thing is clear: God works in the face of our imperfect faith. One year before Isaac was born, Sarah had laughed at the thought that she would conceive and give birth to a son. She had doubted God's word. Yet the New Testament writer of Hebrews tells us that Sarah was "enabled to bear children" by her faith (11:11). Apparently, Sarah's faith was something like

a roller coaster, down one second and up the next. We can certainly identify with her, can't we? In this we see that the Lord can work through imperfect faith, fulfilling his promises through imperfect people!

The Test (Genesis 22)

Two thousand years after Abraham walked the earth, one of his descendants would write a letter reminding the first followers of Jesus that faith without works is dead (James 2:17). As he wrote those words, James was no doubt thinking of his ancestor Abraham. Although Abraham's faith could sometimes waver, we nevertheless see that Abraham had a persistent confidence that God would never break his promise coupled with a willingness to obey God's commands to him. The author of Hebrews tells us that Abraham obeyed God's command to sacrifice his son Isaac because he was confident that God could raise the dead. Abraham believed God's promise that *through Isaac* the covenant promises would be established. Abraham knew that regardless of what God was asking him to do, he would be faithful to keep his promises. And so he obeyed God *in faith.*

Israel Established (Genesis 32–33, 35)

Just as God's choice of an older man and barren woman to birth his chosen people seems strange, so does his determination to use people like Jacob. From a young age, Jacob was known as a trickster, a "grasper" who constantly sought his own good, even at the expense of others (Gen. 25:29–34). Yet God pursued Jacob, wrestling with him along the banks of the Jabbok River, and called him by a new name—Israel.

Discussion Questions

1. "God's will is lived forward and understood backward." What do you think this statement means? How does it reflect the truth of Abraham's life? How have you seen this to be true in your life?

2. What kind of consequences did Abraham and Sarah face for trying to make God's plan work for him? Have you experienced negative consequences from trying to make what you perceived to be God's plan happen on your own? Explain.

3

JOSEPH
From Slave to Deputy Pharaoh

Plot Points

- Through the story of Joseph and his brothers, we discover that God's good plans are *always* brought to pass.
- God remains faithful to his covenant promises, saving his chosen people from famine and using Joseph to save all of Egypt.

Cast of Characters

Benjamin. Israel and Rachel's second-born son; Joseph's younger brother; name means "son of the right hand," indicating a blessed child.

Ephraim. Joseph's second-born son; adopted by Israel so Joseph's line would receive a double portion; name means "making fruitful," indicating Joseph's blessed life in Egypt.

Israel. Married to Leah and Rachel; father of twelve sons who became the twelve tribes of Israel; originally named Jacob ("he takes by the heel" or "he cheats"); name changed to "Israel" ("strives with God") after a wrestling match with God; distraught after Joseph, his favorite son, disappears under apparently violent circumstances.

The Chosen Family (2200–1800 B.C.)

Biblical	Secular
1991 Abraham dies	2106–1786 The Middle Kingdom, a period of renaissance and growth in Egypt.
1915 Rachel gives birth to Joseph	2000 Epic of Gilgamesh records the Sumerian flood legend.
1898 Joseph sold into Egypt	
1886 Isaac dies	
1876 Jacob and family settle in Egypt	1878–1843 Sesostris III is Pharaoh in Egypt. By conservative estimates, he raised Joseph to prominence in Egypt.
1859 Jacob dies	
1805 Joseph dies	1792–1750 Hammurabi rules in Babylon, enacting his famous law code.

Joseph. Israel's favored son, the first child born to Rachel; interpreter of dreams; sold into slavery by his brothers; thrown into an Egyptian prison; raised to second in command by the pharaoh and able to save many from famine.

Judah. Israel's son; Reuben's brother; Joseph's half brother; name means "praise."

Manasseh. Joseph's firstborn son; adopted by Israel so Joseph's line would receive a double portion; name means "making to forget," indicating the joy Joseph found despite his separation from his family.

Pharaoh. May have been Sesostris III, a ruler in the Middle Kingdom period.

Potiphar. Held an important position in Pharaoh's court; oversaw the imprisonment of high officials; name means "bull of Africa."

Reuben. Israel's oldest son; Joseph's half brother; stopped his brothers from murdering Joseph but unable to keep them from sending him into slavery; chastised by his father for his sexual sin; name means "see, a son," an expression of Leah's hope that Israel would love her.

Simeon. Israel and Leah's son; Joseph's half brother; held in ransom until Joseph's brothers returned to Egypt a second time; name sounds like the Hebrew word for "heard," indicating the Lord heard Leah's prayer.

Chapter Overview

One of the central themes of the Old Testament is that God keeps his covenant — his promises to his people. Whether extending his hand of blessing or the rod of judgment, at every point God works to fulfill his covenant promises to Abraham. He promised to make a great nation of Abraham's descendants, giving them a Promised Land, and through them, to bless all nations on earth. In the life of Joseph, one of Abraham's grandsons, we see the great lengths to which God will go to preserve his chosen people and bring his promises to fulfillment.

The story of Joseph is about more than just one person; it is the story of an entire nation, the future people of Israel. As Joseph lived through year after year enduring slavery, imprisonment, and eventually, a rise to a position of governance and blessing, it may have been hard for him to discern God's purposes. However, through it all, we see that God was

Joseph's journey.

working to fulfill the promises made in Joseph's prophetic dreams to safeguard Israel. Although the growing family of Abraham's descendants never could have known in advance, a regional famine was on its way. Little did the brothers realize that by selling their brother into slavery, God would turn their act of jealous hatred into a way of salvation for his people.

In this chapter we see that God's plans cannot be thwarted by sinful humans. In the end even the rebellious and selfish actions of God's enemies are part of God's mysterious will at work in the redemption and salvation of his people. They may intend their actions for evil purposes, but God's good purpose will ultimately triumph.

This silver cup from the Early Bronze Age, discovered near Bethel, depicts a near-Eastern Creation myth, possibly the Enuma Elish.

Z. Radovan/www.BibleLandPictures.com

Section Commentary

Family Troubles (Genesis 37)

You won't get too far in reading through the Old Testament before realizing that polygamy (marriage with multiple wives) is a common part of the story. Jacob married Leah *and* Rachel *and* shared their maids, Bilah and Zilpah. Kings Saul, David, and Solomon each had multiple wives. Yet the New Testament clearly teaches monogamy. Does this mean that the Bible contradicts itself? Are there conflicting messages here? Although a surface reading might lead us to see contradictions, we need to notice that Jesus founds his teaching on monogamy by going back to the beginning — Genesis 2:23 – 24 (see Matt. 19:4 and Mark 10:6). The clearest response to the question of polygamy in the Old Testament is that these believers were not faithful to God's original intention for marriage, yet God still used them despite their imperfections and sinful accommodation to the culture of their day.

Still, all sin has its consequences, and the fruit of their unfaithfulness in marriage is seen everywhere throughout the Old Testament. The practice of polygamy brought ungodly tension and competition between wives, and this tension was often passed on to the children. In Genesis 37 and in later stories, we see the effects of this God-dishonoring practice in the lives of Jacob's children.

Into Egypt (Genesis 37, 39)

For more than thirty centuries, Egypt was the ruling power of the ancient world. From 3000 to 300 B.C., thirty dynasties ruled along the banks of the Nile. Historians divide Egypt's history into seven epochs: Archaic, Old Kingdom,

First Intermediate, Middle Kingdom, Second Intermediate, New Kingdom, and the Late Period (in decline). In that time Egypt's rulers, the pharaohs, functioned as the center of culture and life and were seen as intermediaries between the gods and human beings. As such, they provided the impetus for great building projects and monumental artifacts.

Both Scripture and external sources confirm that Egypt interacted with much of the ancient Near East. Abraham sought relief from famine in Egypt.

The Book of the Dead showing seven cows, similar to Joseph's interpretation of Pharaoh's dream.

Joseph was sold as a slave but raised as a ruler, and his policies saved his own family from famine.

True Dreams (Genesis 41)

Egyptian sources testify to the fact that dreams were taken seriously by all people, commoners and nobles alike, for their ability to reveal secrets and unlock the future. Entire books were written by scribes to help people interpret the meaning of their dreams. In fact, Spell 148 in the *Book of the Dead* touches on the motif of seven cows. In the ancient world, dreams were frequently cited as sufficient rationale for undertaking a particular course of action.

Throughout Scripture we encounter kings who dream: the Egyptian pharaoh, King Nebuchadnezzar of Babylon, and King Xerxes of Persia. In the New Testament, we learn that the wife of the Roman governor of Judea, Pilate, dreamed of Jesus the night before his trial (Matt. 27:19). In each case, the dream is of special import, for when rulers dream it can change the future of a nation — and the world.

A Dream Fulfilled (Genesis 42–48)

Joseph had finally emerged from his dark days of slavery and imprisonment. Ironically, his own dreams were fulfilled by helping others interpret their dreams. For Joseph's brothers, coming face-to-face with their brother was an earth-shaking encounter. He was no longer the little brother they could push around, but a powerful ruler who could have them thrown into a dark place or consigned to lives of slavery.

But Joseph had not harbored a desire for vengeance. Despite their worries, his brothers really had nothing to fear. The same perspective that had sustained Joseph through his most difficult trials now guided his response to them. Joseph's belief that God was in charge freed him to forgive his brothers and was the key to understanding God's greater plan for the family of Abraham.

Discussion Questions

1. What are some of the things the Lord may have worked into Joseph's life through his many years of struggle? What were some of the doubts he may have faced? What can you learn from his example?

2. In effect Joseph said to his brothers, "What you meant for evil, God meant for good." Have you ever had an experience where, looking back, you can see God bringing good out of a sinful choice or an evil act?

DELIVERANCE

4

Plot Points

- God never forgets his promises or his people, and he responds when they cry out for help.
- Although humans might be awed by the power of earthly empires, pharaohs are no match for God's mighty power, demonstrated by the ten plagues of judgment on Egypt.
- The Passover provides a clear picture of the sacrificial lamb as an atonement for the nation of Israel, prefiguring Christ's sacrifice on the cross for the people of God.
- God wants his people to see his acts of deliverance so that they will remember them and know that he can be trusted to keep his promises in the future.

The Deliverance (1525–1450 B.C.)

Late Bronze Age (1550–1200 B.C.)

Biblical	Secular
1526 Moses born 1446 The exodus, crossing of the Red Sea	1648–1540 Hyksos rule in Egypt 1550–1069 The New Kingdom 1550–1525 Ahmose I, pharaoh in Egypt during a period of intense nationalism; reign of the foreign Hyksos finally brought to an end 1525–1504 Amenhotep I 1504–1492 Thutmose I 1492–1479 Thutmose II 1478–1457 Hatshepsut 1479–1425 Thutmose III extends Egypt's reach into Syria

This wall painting from the Dura Europos—one of the earliest known synagogues, dating to approximately A.D. 245—shows Pharaoh's daughter and the infant Moses.

Z. Radovan/www.BibleLandPictures.com

Cast of Characters

Aaron. A Levite; the first high priest; Moses' brother; used by the Lord to help Moses convey God's word to Pharaoh; name means "a teacher."

Gershom. Moses' first son; name means "a stranger here."

I AM. God reveals his name, Yahweh, the LORD; comes from the Hebrew verb "to be"; indicates God as the one who "is" and the one "who causes to be," in other words, the Creator.

Miriam. Moses' sister; her quick thinking helped reconnect infant Moses with his mother; traveled with Israel into freedom and across the desert; name means "rebellion."

Moses. Called by God to lead Israel from slavery in Egypt to freedom in the Promised Land; saved from death by a brave mother and father; raised in the house of Pharaoh; called from tending sheep in the desert to leading God's people through it; name sounds like the Hebrew "to draw out," indicating Moses being taken out of the Nile by Pharaoh's daughter, also commonly used in Egyptian names meaning "to father" or "to be fathered."

Pharaoh. Ruler in Egypt during the confrontation with Moses and freeing of Israel; possibly Thutmose III.

Pharaoh. Ruler in Egypt to whom "Joseph meant nothing" (Ex. 1:8); scholars are divided as to his identity.

Reuel. Priest of Midian; Moses' father-in-law; also called Jethro ("his excellence"); name means "the shepherd or friend of God."

Zipporah. Daughter of Reuel; Moses' first wife; mother of Gershom and Eliezer; name means "beauty."

Chapter Overview

Egypt was the major power of the ancient world. The pharaohs left behind great pyramids, building projects, and large-scale artistic works. Contrast the archaeological heritage of this great empire with the historical artifacts from the nation of Israel. If set on a scale, Egypt would clearly be the winner.

Yet in terms of long-term impact, no other people have affected the course of human history like the people of Israel, the Jews. The God who saved them in the Exodus is still worshiped today, while the gods of the pharaohs are now nothing more than artifacts in museums. In this story of deliverance, God reveals himself as the mover of empires with authority over the kings of the earth. Israel discovered that their Lord was much more than a regional, tribal deity. His power could not be matched by any other god.

Section Commentary

The Pharaoh Who Forgot
(Exodus 1 – 2)

What is the setting for this amazing story? While it is difficult to establish an exact historical timeline, the story of Exodus suggests that Egypt had finally emerged from under the leadership of a foreign people who had ruled Lower Egypt for more than one hundred years, the Hyksos. This could help to explain the antagonism toward the Hebrews, the descendants of Abraham, shown by the Egyptian pharaoh in the story. This is a significant shift from the days of Joseph when God's people were welcomed and enjoyed a position of favor. Egyptian military power was now at its peak, and

the land had been recently united under a new dynasty. The pharaoh "to whom Joseph meant nothing" (1:8) may have been Seti I. His son, Rameses II continued his father's building program, including the building of great "store cities" (for storing arms and provisions), perhaps using Israelite slaves to do this work.

Built for Pharaoh Seti, the Temple of Abydos is dedicated to Osiris, the Egyptian god of the underworld. This is a view of the chapel pledged to the god Amun.

© Amanda Lewis/www.istockphoto.com

God in the Wasteland (Exodus 2 – 4)

God is determined to reveal himself. We see this theme everywhere in the Scriptures. At the burning bush, God gives Moses one of the most profound glimpses of his essential nature ever recorded. Moses encounters a God who is holy, who responds to his people's needs and yet is also transcendent. God shares his name with Moses: "I AM."

In ancient cultures names carried great significance. Often something about a name revealed a character quality or detail about that person. We have seen this already in the names of various Old Testament characters (see Cast of Characters). To this day the precise meaning of *YHWH* is unclear to us, but we do know that it is somehow related to the verb "to be." In other words, God wants us to know that God is who he is. God is who he will be. And he is the one who brings things into being. These are all possible renderings of his powerful name, I AM.

The Confrontation (Exodus 5 – 11)

It is nearly impossible to overstate the faith-shaking effect the ten plagues must have had on the Egyptian people. Each plague put one of their deities in the cross-hairs and brought it down.

Through his judgments, God was not only punishing Pharaoh for his disobedience, he was asserting his power and authority over the Egyptian gods, destroying the very foundations of Egyptian power and rule.

Scala/Art Resource, NY

An Egyptian wall painting from the tomb of Thutmosis IV that shows representations of the Egyptian gods Anubis and Hathor.

Plague	Scripture	Egyptian gods
Nile turned to blood	Ex. 7:14 – 25	**Hapi and Isis:** god and goddess of the Nile **Osiris:** Nile served as bloodstream
Frogs	Ex. 8:1 – 15	**Haget:** goddess of birth with a frog head
Gnats	Ex. 8:16 – 19	**Set:** god of the desert
Flies	Ex. 8:20 – 32	**Re:** sun god **Uatchit:** possibly represented by a fly
Death of livestock	Ex. 9:1 – 7	**Hathor:** goddess with cow head **Apis:** the bull god
Boils	Ex. 8 – 12	**Sekhmet:** goddess of disease **Sunu:** pestilence god **Imhotep:** god of medicine
Hail	Ex. 9:13 – 35	**Nut:** sky goddess **Set:** god of storms
Locusts	Ex. 10:1 – 20	**Osiris:** god of crops and fertility
Darkness	Ex. 10:21 – 29	**Re:** the sun god **Horus:** a sun god
Death of the firstborn	Ex. 11:1 – 12:36	**Min:** god of reproduction **Isis:** goddess who protected children Pharaoh's firstborn son, a god

Deliverance, Danger, Desert
(Exodus 12 – 17)

When God called Moses to confront Pharaoh, he referred to Israel as his "firstborn son" (Ex. 4:22). For far too long, Pharaoh had held this son in captivity. Pharaoh had ignored God's clear warning. Now Pharaoh would lose his firstborn son for threatening the life of God's firstborn son.

The story of the Passover sacrifice lies at the heart of the Old Testament story. By God's command the events of that night were memorialized in annual celebration. The blood of the lamb made God's people safe from his judgment. Pharaoh's hardened heart was broken when his firstborn son was taken, and God displayed his unswerving commitment to save his son in a miraculous escape through the parting of the waters at the Red Sea. It is a story of redemption and deliverance that lays the foundation for an even greater story of redemption and deliverance yet to come through the sacrifice of God's firstborn Son on a cross.

Discussion Questions

1. "Always remember!" is a recurring theme in Scripture. God called the Israelites regularly to celebrate festivals in which they recounted the stories of God's work in their lives. What stories of God's power at work in your life could you repeat more often?

2. As you consider the life of Moses, several parallels between him and Jesus emerge. Can you list some of them? What is the significance of this overlap?

5

NEW COMMANDS
AND A NEW COVENANT

Plot Points

• God presents his people with his commands, outlining his expectations for the covenant community.

• God's central desire is to have a people with whom he can dwell in relationship and through whom he can reveal himself to the world.

Cast of Characters

Aaron. A Levite; the first high priest; Moses' brother; used by the Lord to help Moses convey God's word to Pharaoh.

Joshua. Son of Nun, an aide to Moses; name means "the Lord saves"; later this Hebrew name would be rendered in Greek as Jesus.

Moses. Called by God to lead Israel from slavery in Egypt to freedom in the Promised Land; saved from death by a brave mother and father; raised in the house of Pharaoh; called from tending sheep in the desert to leading God's people through it; called a friend of God; Israel's great lawgiver.

The Deliverance (1525 – 1450 B.C.)

Biblical	Secular
1446 The exodus, crossing of the Red Sea	1479 – 1425 Thutmose III extends Egypt's reach into Syria.
1406 Moses dies, Joshua is appointed leader, Israelites enter Canaan	1460 – 1200 Neo-Hittite Empire

Chapter Overview

When Moses first approached Pharaoh, he asked that God's people be allowed to travel to the desert to worship their God. At last, after an extraordinary confrontation and a miraculous escape, that time had come. The Lord God met with the people of Israel at Mount Sinai and over a period of time revealed to them his covenant promises and the laws and commands that would guide and shape their identity as a nation. From the burning branches of a bush on that same mountain, he had called Moses into ministry. Now, with the entire mountain aflame in the fire of his glorious presence, he extends that call to the entire nation.

For eleven months Israel camped at Sinai. Their actions during that time proved to be a microcosm of their future life as a nation. In one breath they affirmed their desire to be a covenant people. But in the next they were bowing down before an Egyptian idol. The nation continues this cycle of sin, repentance, and renewal throughout their time in the desert. In these sections, as God reveals the Law to Israel and details the construction of the tabernacle, he demonstrates his commitment to make these people his own. They would be his people and he their God.

Section Commentary

At Mount Sinai (Exodus 19)

The location of Mount Sinai is a matter of some debate. Three separate regions offer possible locations: northwest Saudi Arabia or south Jordan, the northern Sinai peninsula, or the highlands of the southern Sinai. Traditionally, Mount Sinai has been linked to the modern Jebal Musa ("mountain of Moses") in southern Sinai, and there are many reasons this is probably the best location.

Much more significant than the debates about where exactly Sinai was, though, is the issue of *what happened there*. In the eleven months Israel camped at Sinai, they witnessed God's glory manifest in flame and thunder on the mountain. Most importantly, it was at Mount Sinai that God gave his law to Israel.

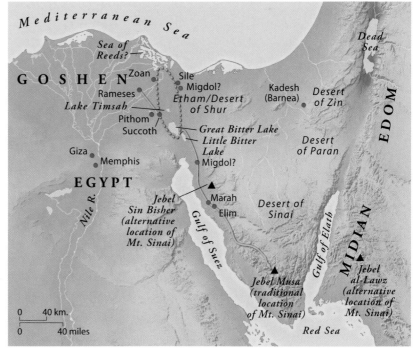

The exodus.

Ten Commandments (Exodus 20)

The Ten Commandments exhibit a particular structure and serve a particular function. Structurally, the Ten Commandments can be divided into two parts, or "tables." Commandments one through four emphasize our relationship with God, the vertical axis. Commandments five through ten emphasize our relationship with other people, the horizontal axis.

Functionally, these commandments serve to help bring conviction into our lives. Honest reflection on the commandments reveals our

Jebel Musa, the traditional location of Mount Sinai.

deep need for God's grace. Jesus himself demonstrated this in his Sermon on the Mount, teaching his followers that obedience to the law was not merely a matter of external, formal observance but a matter of the heart. The spiritual nature of God's law underlies its convicting power to reveal our hidden sins and acts of disobedience.

Some of the Reformers taught that the law had another function: providing not only conviction, but instruction to God's people. Each of the commands carries not simply a "thou shalt not," but an implicit, "thou shalt." For instance, the command not to covet our neighbor's possessions, when really understood, calls us to live a life of radical generosity.

Worshipers Called Out (Exodus 24 – 25)

Exodus 24 and 25 are the last and first chapters, respectively, of two key sections of Scripture. Chapter 24 closes a series of commands that make up what is commonly called "The Book of the Covenant." These laws, committed to writing, spelled out what it meant to be the Hebrew nation. As a nation, Israel confirmed their intention to live according to this covenant. Chapter 25 opens up seven chapters on the construction of the tabernacle. Moses was called up to the mountain for forty days and forty nights to receive these instructions. In essence, the people learned *how* they should live if they were to live in the presence of a holy God. Then Moses learned how to build the place in which that holy God would live in their midst.

The Golden Calf (Exodus 32)

Exodus 21 through 31 describes an ideal situation. The Lord reveals his covenantal expectations. The Israelites affirm their desire to live in covenant. Then Moses spends forty days learning the design and method for building the tabernacle. But just forty days after Israel has confirmed its intentions, the people build an idol and run wild. Sadly, this was a portent of things to come again and again and again and....

God with Us (Exodus 33 – 34, 40)

The Story is held together with a few key narrative threads. These threads can be traced throughout every part of the book from beginning to end. One of the most important threads is that God wants to live with his people. This was his desire in Eden. It was represented in the tabernacle and later the temple. In the New Testament, we learn that God, rather than inhabiting structures of stone and wood, inhabits the flesh and blood fellowship of the church. Of course, one day he really will return to live with his people in the new heavens and new earth. We will see him as he is, and we will live with him in perfect fellowship.

Moses was called up to Mount Sinai to receive instructions on how to build the tabernacle.

Discussion Questions

1. In the wilderness, God presented himself in thunder, lightning, and flame on a mountain that could not be touched. What does this tell us about God's character? Are these things true today? What other images does God use to describe his presence in Scripture?

2. What role do the Ten Commandments play in your life with God? Should and/or how can they play a more significant role?

3. Why do you think it was so easy for Israel to slip from covenant affirmation to idolatry? What, if anything, should we learn from this?

6 WANDERING

Plot Points

- The Lord is looking for followers who will passionately honor and trust him.
- Israel's constant grumbling elicits God's wrath.
- Israel evaluated God's commands according to their limited perspective, disobeying God and refusing to take the land, condemning an entire generation to death in the desert.
- Moses' years of faithful obedience did not give him license to disobey, even once.
- Our ability to live faithfully before the Lord is directly tied to our *constantly remembering* God's Word.

Cast of Characters

Aaron. Served the Lord as high priest in Israel's desert wanderings; died on Mount Hor after handing over his ministry to his son Eleazar.

Baal of Peor. Baal is mentioned in this passage for the first time in the Old Testament; one of the chief Canaanite deities; triumphs over sea, death, and Leviathan with the help of his consort, Anath; chief competitor to Yahweh in the hearts and minds of Israel.

Balaam. Pagan diviner, called to curse the Israelites but blesses them instead; name means "the ancient of the people, the destruction of the people."

The Deliverance (1525 – 1450 B.C.)

Biblical	Secular
1446 The exodus, crossing of the Red Sea	1550 – 1069 The New Kingdom — Egypt
1406 Moses dies, Joshua is appointed leader, Israelites enter Canaan	1460 – 1200 Neo-Hittite Empire
	1479 – 1425 Pharaoh Thutmose III
	1427 – 1400 Pharaoh Amenhotep II

Balak. Ruler of Moab, a tribal confederation; attempts to curse Israel; name means "who lays waste or destroys."

Caleb. Son of Jephunneh; sent on a reconnaissance mission into Canaan and came back with a faith-filled heart, convinced that the Lord's power was sufficient to lead them to victory; name means "dog."

Eleazar. Son of Aaron; anointed as high priest when his father died on Mount Hor; name means "help of God."

Joshua. Son of Nun, an aide to Moses; name means "the Lord saves"; later this Hebrew name would be rendered in Greek as Jesus.

King of Arad. Unknown historical figure; may have ruled from the city of Hormah.

Miriam. Served the Lord in the exodus and in the desert wanderings; died at Kadesh in the Desert of Zin.

Moses. Led God's chosen people through the wilderness to the edge of the Promised Land then died on Mount Nebo.

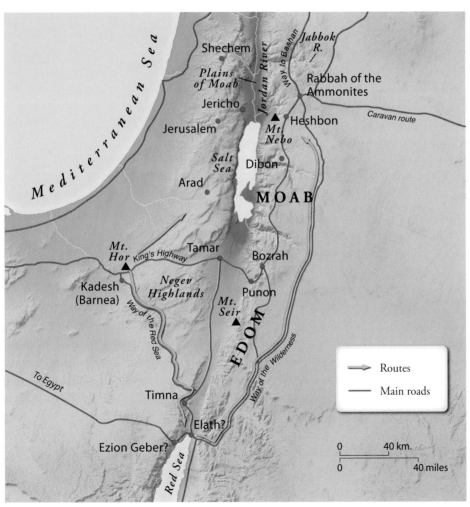

Wilderness wanderings.

Og. King of Bashan; ruled from Ashtaroth, near the Yarmuk River; his kingdom was decimated in the Israelite invasion.

Phinehas. Son of Eleazar, grandson of Aaron the high priest; takes decisive action against two idolaters, averting God's wrath and achieving a perpetual priesthood; name means "bold aspect."

Sihon. King of the Amorites, an ethnic group occupying the Transjordan region; name means "rooting out."

This Roman catacomb wall painting shows Moses striking the rock.

Chapter Overview

For more than a year, Israel camped at Mount Sinai. Every day they saw evidence of God's reality and power. They were saved from their idolatry, building the tabernacle and seeing God's presence fill it. After all this, one would think they could walk faithfully before the Lord, but sadly, that is not what happened.

Following hard on the heels of their departure from Sinai, Israel descended into constant grumbling. They went back and forth between complaining about their circumstances and asking God to help them and rescue them from their struggles. God was not very tolerant of their ungrateful rabble-rousing and constant complaints.

Even worse, after finally reaching the Promised Land the people refused to step forward in faith and trust that God would lead them. When the Lord called them to take the land through wars of conquest, they flatly refused. As a result an entire generation was condemned to death in the desert. During the desert years, God shaped and formed a man named Joshua into a capable successor to Moses.

After forty years of wandering, as Israel approached their inheritance a second time, Moses, the great lawgiver, gave his farewell address, holding out the choice between life and death, blessings and curses. What is revealed in all these ups and downs? God is the glorious, faithful, covenant-keeping Savior of his chosen people — despite their constant disobedience and sin.

Section Commentary

The Rabble (Numbers 10–12)

The greatest enemy of faith is forgetfulness. All too often we forget just how bad slavery is. It is easy to criticize the Israelites for wanting to go back to Egypt, but how often do we look with longing at things we know deep down have always led to heartache? We also forget just how faithful the Lord has been to us. Israel had seen God's awesome deliverance. They had seen him work wonders in Egypt. But when times got rough, their forgetfulness led them to minimize both the horror of slavery and the goodness of God.

A Crisis of Faith (Numbers 13–14, 20)

Again and again, God asks Israel a simple question: Do you trust me? Do you trust me to provide you with food and drink? Do you trust me to give you victory against your enemies?

As Israel stood at the border of the Promised Land, they were one step away from experiencing the fulfillment of God's amazing promise to Abraham. Five hundred years earlier, Abraham had been a desert wanderer, just like Israel. But now the Lord had led them to their inheritance. Sadly, they did not have the same faith as their ancestor before them.

Fighting Battles (Numbers 21, 25)

Israel had two different battles to fight. First, they faced the swords of the attacking armies. Historians have not yet determined the identity of the kings mentioned here, but we can get some idea of what they were like. They were likely warlords and tribal leaders who controlled many of the regions through which Israel had to travel. Although their influence was limited to

A bronze figurine from the tenth century B.C. reminiscent of Balaam.

Z. Radovan/www.BibleLandPictures.com

a small geographic area, they were nevertheless capable of coordinating their efforts against a common enemy.

Enemy armies were not the only foes Israel encountered. The greater battle lay within, a battle warring for the allegiance of their hearts. The people of Israel repeatedly squared off against the constant temptation of idolatry. This battle, as we will see, was one they all too often lost. Even as the Lord was delivering the nation from the curses of the Moabite king Balak, the Israelites were embracing Moabite religion and making ritual prostitution a part of their worship. The example of Phinehas shows us that the battle against idolatry requires the same level of passion and commitment as the fight against an armed enemy.

Transitions (Numbers 27; Deuteronomy 1–2, 4, 6, 8–9, 29–32, 34)

As Moses hands the leadership of Israel over to Joshua, Israel's faithful leader shares some final, parting words with the people he has led for many long years. Moses speaks about God's covenant, reminding the people of their identity and their unique calling as the chosen people of God. Like other ancient Near Eastern covenants, the covenant between God and Israel had a clear structure:

Ancient Treaty Structure	Deuteronomy
Preamble	1:1–5
Historical prologue	1:6–4:49
General stipulations	5:1–11:32
Specific stipulations	12:1–26:19
Blessings and curses	27:1–28:68
Document clause	31:9–29
Witnesses	32:1–47

From *ESV Study Bible*, introduction to Deuteronomy.

Discussion Questions

1. Why do you think it is often easier to grumble than to remain grateful?

2. What are some key characteristics of Moses' approach to leadership? (List at least three and provide examples.)

3. Moses called the people of Israel to a life of obedience, promising that life and blessing would flow from it. With such a clear blessing extended to us, we still find it difficult to remain obedient. What role does "remembrance" have in remaining faithful?

THE BATTLE BEGINS

7

Plot Points

• Israel is given a second chance to do what they failed to do the first time they stood at the border of the Promised Land — trust the Lord to bring victory as they walk in faithful obedience.

• God brings ethnic outsiders who demonstrate faith in the God of Israel into his covenant community.

• Israel is called to bring God's judgment on Canaan by completely cleansing the land of its former occupants.

• Israel is called to be a people led and directed by God's revelation, through the Book of the Law and regular prayer.

The Promised Land (1400–1000 B.C.)

Biblical	Secular
1406 Moses dies, Joshua is appointed leader, Israelites enter Canaan 1406–1375 Conquest of Canaan 1375 Joshua dies 1375–1050 Time of the judges	1460–1200 Neo-Hittite Empire 1365–1275 Assyrian kings Assur-uballit I and Adad-nirari I reassert Assyrian dominance in the region, casting off the Mitanni rule. The Mitanni may have been among the first oppressors of Israel in the judges era. 1352–1336 Pharaoh Amenhotep IV changes his name to Akhenaten and attempts a reform of Egyptian religion, seeking monotheistic worship of Aten, the sun god. 1239–1213 Egypt enacts great building programs under the rule of Seti I and Rameses II

Cast of Characters

Achan. An Israelite who ignored the Lord's command that all Jericho should be devoted to destruction; brought death on himself and all his family as a result; name is the Hebrew word for "disaster."

Adoni-Zedek. Like Melchizedek, a king of Jerusalem; name means "lord of righteousness."

Amorite kings. Hoham of Hebron, Piram of Jarmuth, Japhia of Lachish, Debir of Eglon; called together by Adoni-Zedek, king of Jerusalem, to attack Gibeon.

Jabin. King of Hazor; formed an alliance to fight Israel; a Middle Bronze Age letter with a similarly named ruler in Hazor indicates this may have been a dynastic name.

Jobab. King of Madon; joined an alliance to battle Israel; name reflects the time and place of Joshua 11.

Joshua. Son of Nun; an aide to Moses; leader of Israel in the conquest; name means "the Lord saves"; later this Hebrew name would be rendered in Greek as Jesus.

Rahab. A prostitute in Jericho who helped two Israelite spies; commended throughout Scripture for her faith; a distant ancestor of Jesus; name means "large, extended."

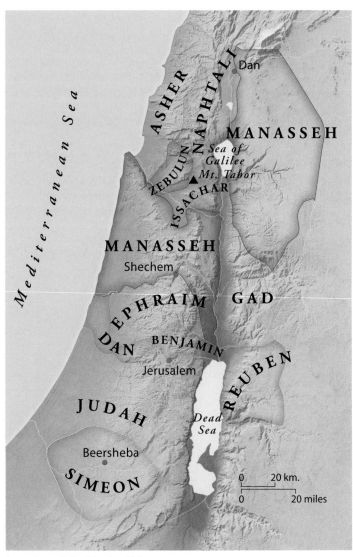

Location of the Twelve Tribes.

Chapter Overview

Joshua must have experienced déjà vu as he entered the Promised Land. He had stood in the same place forty years earlier and watched as Israel had turned away from their inheritance. The challenge God had given them — to take the land — had not changed, but the people of Israel had. The former, faithless generation had passed away, and a new generation had arisen, ready and willing to be led into the Promised Land.

Some key themes emerge as the people enter the land of promise. First, it is clear that the Lord, not the strength of Israel's army, will make victory possible. The very first battle they fight is won with the sound of trumpets! Second, their mission demands a heart of courage. While the Lord promises to go before Israel, he still calls them to fight bravely. Their courage, however, is more than foolish enthusiasm; it is rooted in the third key theme: trust and obedience. If Israel has any hope of achieving victory, they must walk in obedience to God's word. The story of Achan demonstrates this lesson clearly.

Central to the conquest of Canaan is the concept of *fulfillment*. The Lord is fulfilling the promise he made to Abraham more than six hundred years earlier. This Promised Land is an inheritance for God's chosen people. But the Lord is also fulfilling his sentence of judgment against the Canaanite people, spoken more than six hundred years earlier when the Lord declared that punishment of their sin was inevitable. Israel is being called to fulfill the Lord's instructions, and they will rise victorious as they do.

Section Commentary

Jericho Falls (Joshua 1 – 2, 6)

Most of the conquest of Canaan did not involve the total destruction of cities. In many cases Israel simply drove out or annihilated the occupants and inhabited existing cities. However, three cities — Jericho, Ai, and Hazor — were the exception. Of these three, Jericho was a special case. It was designated as a city "devoted to the Lord." Even before the Israelite invasion, Jericho had a long history of immorality and idolatry.

While the actual date of Jericho's fall is disputable, there is some archaeological data that may correspond to the biblical account. Jericho was a well-known, wealthy city with massive defenses. A fifteen-foot stone wall was

Asherah, the Canaanite goddess of fertility, was worshiped as a house deity, 10th to 7th century B.C.

Z. Radovan/www.BibleLandPictures.com

Evidence suggests that Jericho had two walls: a lower mud brick wall, built on top of this revetment wall, and an upper wall, located higher up on the mound.

topped by a mud brick wall six feet thick and eighteen to twenty-four feet high. These massive walls collapsed at the base, forming a ramp for an invading army. Evidence indicates that the city fell during the harvest season, precisely when Joshua records Israel's victory to have taken place. While many archaeological questions remain, these are undoubtedly interesting discoveries that correlate with the biblical account.

Achan and Ai (Joshua 8)

Two interesting story lines intersect at Jericho. Achan, an Israelite by birth, had just witnessed the miraculous toppling of Jericho's walls, yet he could not keep his hands off the treasure that had been devoted to the Lord. Because he directly disobeyed a command of God, he was taken "outside the camp" with his family and stoned to death.

Contrasting with this story of judgment on a disobedient Israelite is the story of Rahab, a Canaanite prostitute who risked her life and that of her family to save two Israelite spies. In addition to her courageous efforts to save the spies, Rahab proclaimed her belief that the Lord was with Israel. By God's gracious acceptance, this outsider became a part of God's chosen people.

Moreover, this former prostitute would become one of the direct ancestors of God's Son, Jesus Christ. The lesson in all of this: nationality is not as important as faithful obedience.

Troublesome Alliances
(Joshua 10 – 11)

We have no way of knowing how the decisions we make will affect our future. Israel's decision to align themselves with the Gibeonite envoys is a case in point. Because Joshua and the Israelite leaders moved forward without consulting the Lord, they were drawn into battle when Gibeon was attacked. And even long after Joshua and the leaders who made the treaty had passed away, Israel would pay the price for breaking their agreement (2 Sam. 21) and suffer through famine. The book of Joshua rings out clearly with this theme: the Lord's way is the only way!

Whom Will You Serve?
(Joshua 23 – 24)

Like Moses before him, Joshua ends his time in leadership with a clear, challenging message to the people. He calls the people to remember what God has done and what he has promised to do. Summoning them together at Shechem, he reminds them of God's call to Abraham. He calls them to remember their deliverance from Egypt and salvation from the kings of Transjordan. And he reminds the people that they must choose for themselves: whom will they serve?

Jesus gave his followers a similar choice in Mark 8:34 – 36:

> Then he called the crowd to him along with his disciples and said: "Whoever wants to be my disciple must deny themselves and take up their cross and follow me. For whoever wants to save their life will lose it, but whoever loses their life for me and for the gospel will save it. What good is it for you to gain the whole world, yet forfeit your soul?"

Discussion Questions

1. In the Canaanite conquest, God used Israel to bring judgment on whole people groups. How does this image of God fit in with the popular understanding of God?

2. Throughout the book of Joshua, there are times when Israel "gets it," following the Lord faithfully, and times when they do not. List a few examples of each. Where do you see yourself in these examples?

3. Having read the story of Joshua and the conquest, respond to this statement: God clearly desires to bless his people and prosper them.

8

A FEW GOOD MEN ... AND WOMEN

Plot Points

- Israel's failure to fully drive out the Canaanites led them into compromise and gross idolatry.
- God's people are constantly caught up in a four-stage cycle: (1) sin, (2) oppression, (3) repentance, (4) deliverance.
- The Lord was willing to use flawed people to bring about his people's deliverance.

Cast of Characters

Barak. Commander of Israel's army and the campaign against Sisera; name means "lightning."

Cushan-Rishathaim. King of Aram Naharaim; dominated Israel for eight years; vanquished by Othniel; name sounds like Hebrew rendering of "Cushan of double wickedness."

Deborah. A judge of Israel; wife of Lappidoth; a prophet; name means "bee."

Delilah. A Philistine; Samson's lover; succeeded in convincing Samson to divulge the secret of his strength, undoing him in the process; name means "poor; small; head of hair."

Eglon. King of Moab; oppressed Israel for eighteen years; name sounds like the Hebrew word for "round" or "rotund."

The Promised Land

Iron Age I (1200–1000 B.C.)

Biblical	Secular
1209–1169 Deborah	1115–1076 Tiglath-pileser I leads Assyrian expansion
1162–1122 Gideon	into Lebanon.
1105 Hannah gives birth to Samuel	1100 Enuma Elish, the Akkadian creation myth
1075–1055 Samson	

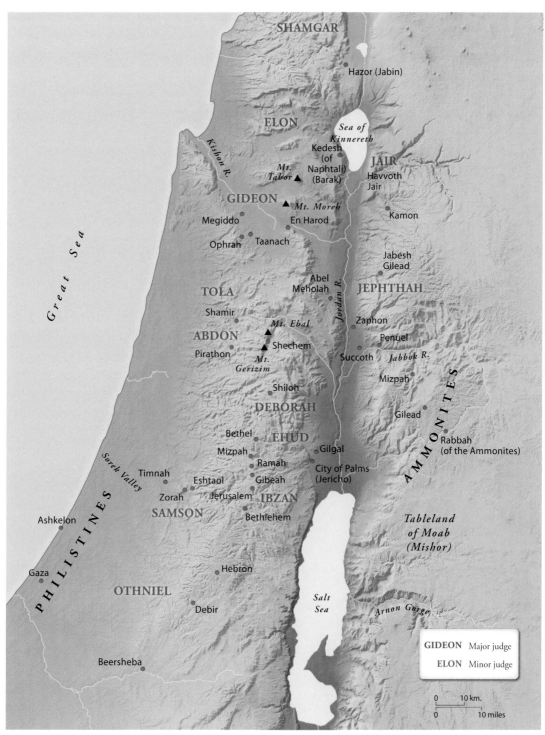

The Judges of Israel.

Ehud. Clever, daring, brave, limping man who assassinated Eglon and led Israel against the Moabites; ushered in eighty peaceful years; name means "Where is the splendor, majesty?"

Gideon (aka Jerub-Baal). A judge of Israel; son of Joash the Abiezrite, a socially insignificant clan; led Israel to victory over Midian, overcoming incredible odds in stunning fashion; name means "he who bruises or breaks, a destroyer."

Jael. Wife of Heber; a daring woman who killed Sisera, violating her husband's peace treaty with Jabin; name means "ibex," a wild mountain goat.

Joash. Father of Gideon; followed Canaanite idolatry, worshiping Baal and Asherah; name means "Yahweh is strong," indicating his parents remembered Yahweh.

Othniel. A judge of Israel; son of Kenaz; Caleb's younger brother; defeated Cushan-Rishathaim, king of Aram; name means "the hour of God."

Purah. Gideon's servant; heard the Midianites' misgivings about the battle.

Samson. A judge of Israel; miraculously given to his barren mother on the condition that he be a Nazirite; lived and died fighting the Philistines; name means "little sun," perhaps indicating the light he brought into the dark time of the judges.

Sisera. Commander of Jabin's army; name is not Semitic, indicating he may have been a Hittite or Hurrian mercenary.

Chapter Overview

If the book of Joshua demonstrates what Israel did right, then the book of Judges shows what they did wrong. A popular definition of insanity is doing the same thing again and again, yet expecting different results. If that is true, then God's people at this time were trapped in madness, living in a cycle of disobedience, crying out to God for help and falling back into patterns of idolatry and sin.

As story after story is recounted, a clear pattern, or "sin cycle," emerges. God's people were perpetually spinning through stages of sin, oppression, repentance, and deliverance. From one generation to the next, their communal identity, centered in the Book of the Law and covenant obedience, was gradually disintegrating. The Lord had called the people of Israel out of the nations to have a distinct voice and presence in the world, but increasingly, God's people looked no different from the world around them.

When we refuse to listen to his Word, God often makes use of circumstances to get our attention. For Israel, the circumstances had to be dire before the people would awaken to just how far they had drifted from their calling. One of the central themes of the story of Scripture is that in the face of our faithlessness, God remains true to his word! He is the God who brings rescue and salvation to his people, and he will even use flawed people to do it.

Section Commentary

Sin Cycle (Judges 2–3)

From one generation to the next, the people forgot the Lord. How could this have happened? Apparently, they had neglected Moses' clear instructions: "These commandments that I give you today are to be on your hearts. Impress them on your children. Talk about them when

Erich Lessing/Art Resource, NY

Deities from the Canaanite High Place at Nahariyah, Late Bronze Age. The Judges expressed God's disappointment to the people, since they had disobeyed him and engaged in idol worship.

you sit at home and when you walk along the road, when you lie down and when you get up" (Deut. 6:6 – 7).

Israel forgot that they were called to be a distinctive, holy people in an unholy culture. They won the land of promise but lost the war against complacency. As a result they were pulled into the "sin cycle" and were trapped by the idolatry of the Canaanites.

As modern readers it can be difficult for us to identify with Israel's attraction to the Baals and Ashtoreths. We easily forget just how countercultural God had called Israel to be. In the world of ancient Israel, each territory had its own gods, and each god had a different function. No single deity could take care of everything, nor would that God expect exclusive worship. When Israel added other pagan gods to their worship of YHWH, they were doing what seemed natural to them.

Deborah and Barak (Judges 4)

The story of Deborah and Barak stands out for many reasons, not least because Deborah is the only female judge mentioned in Scripture. The story also records historical details that have been confirmed by archaeologists in recent years. We read that Deborah and Barak defeated Jabin, ruler at Hazor. Excavations at Hazor have provided evidence of massive destruction that happened during Deborah and Barak's time. In fact, the heads and hands of idols and statues of dignitaries appear to have been intentionally cut off and removed. Consider this in light of Moses' instruction in Deuteronomy 12:3 that God's people "cut down the idols of [the nations'] gods."

God's Prophet (Judges 6)

Israel was feeling the heavy hand of God's judgment. Scripture tells us Midianites invaded like a swarm of locusts. Why would the Scriptures record the invasion of a foreign army using this metaphor? Consider that in 1957 a swarm of locusts in Somaliland was estimated to number 16 billion and weigh fifty thousand tons. Each locust would consume its own weight in vegetation each day, so a swarm of locusts would completely devastate a region.

Samson slaying a Philistine.

The writer is showing us that the Israelites were experiencing the devastating effects of their own sin through God's judgments against them.

Into this situation, however, the Lord sent his prophet as a gift of grace to his people. Throughout Israel's history the prophet played a key role. He reminded the people of who God was, what he had done, and what he was able to do. He applied God's revelation to a contemporary situation and sometimes spoke a God-given glimpse of events to come. Ultimately, he called the people to true repentance, turning away from their sin and abandoning their idolatry — more than a simple cry for deliverance and help.

Gideon (Judges 6 – 8)

The story of Gideon is packed with interesting details. For instance, his father's name, Joash, means "YHWH is strong." Sadly, although his father's name hinted at a deep faith in God, the truth was that Gideon's father was an idolater who erected an altar to Baal and an image of Asherah. When the angel of the Lord comes to see Gideon, he is threshing his grain in a winepress. Usually people threshed their grain on a hilltop to allow the wind to blow away the chaff. But working in such a visible location would have let everyone, including the Midianites, see that Gideon had grain to steal. So, instead, Gideon hides his work from prying eyes in a winepress, a sign of his fear and cowardice. Later in the story, we see Gideon placing a fleece, apparently in an attempt to discern God's will. But a closer reading of the passage shows that this was not his intent. We read that Gideon had been given a clear command by God. He was simply trying to find a way to get out of it! Gideon is a flawed man with an idolatrous past who struggles with fear and is inclined toward disobedience of God's commands.

Yet like all the stories in the book of Judges, Gideon's tale emphasizes the mixed-up world of this era. Judges is a book with very few examples of faith-filled champions. In most cases the Lord works with fearful, sinful, and selfish "heroes" to get the job done. But that shouldn't surprise us, because God works with us as well! Gideon did one thing exactly right: he kept walking forward into God's will.

Samson and the Philistines
(Judges 13 – 16)

The Philistines were known in the ancient world as "the sea people." Originating in Crete, this nation swept into Canaan and pushed on toward conquering Egypt to establish a new empire. But Rameses III, the Egyptian Pharaoh, turned them back. Nevertheless, the Philistines were still able to establish a federation of five city-states in the land of Canaan: Ashdod, Ashkelon, Ekron, Gath, and Gaza. Their presence in the land was a constant threat and a source of irritation to the people of Israel. God's central call on Samson's life was to fight against them.

Discussion Questions

1. Why do you think we too often take God's blessings for granted and slip into indifference, complacency, or even sin?

2. Many of the judges were seriously flawed. What do we learn about God in the fact that he still used these people?

3. What are some of the idols in our contemporary culture? Which do you find difficult to eradicate from your life?

9

THE FAITH OF A FOREIGN WOMAN

Plot Points

- Though born and raised in a pagan culture, Ruth the Moabite emerges as a shining example of loyalty and faith.
- Against the backdrop of Israel's unfaithfulness, Boaz stands out as a generous and faithful kinsman-redeemer.
- Despite the bitter loss of her husband and sons, Naomi is embraced and safeguarded by an unlikely family.

Israel and Moab

Born of the incestuous relationship between Lot and his daughter, Moab represented a constant threat to the Israelites. In every way, they embodied the dangers and temptations God wanted Israel to eschew. And yet, it was a Moabite named Ruth who would stand in direct relation to Jesus. This chart (on page 53) examines the Biblical history of Israel and Moab.

STORIES OF CONFLICT: Throughout the OT, Israel and Moab were in constant military conflict.

STORIES OF COMPROMISE: Though Israel was called to be holy and set apart, we find her constantly compromising this call in favor of other gods, including those of Moab.

WORDS OF CONDEMNATION: God spoke through His prophets not only to Israel, but also to nations around her. Moab was addressed many times in prophetic literature.

The Promised Land
Iron Age I (1200–1000 B.C.)

Biblical	Secular
1162–1122 Gideon: Ruth most likely lived during the judgeship of Gideon	1115–1076 Tiglath-pileser I leads Assyrian expansion into Lebanon

Stories of Conflict	Stories of Compromise	Words of Condemnation
Numbers 22–24 As the Israelites approach the Promised Land, the Moabites enlist Balaam to curse God's people. Ironically, each attempt to curse results instead in blessing! (Cf. Jos. 24:9–10; Mic. 6:5.)	*Genesis 19:37* Moab is born through the incestuous relations of Lot and his daughter.	*Deuteronomy 23:3* The LORD forbids any Moabite to enter the Temple.
Judges 3 God delivers Israel from Moabite oppression through Ehud's daring assassination of Moab's king.	*Numbers 25* Just as God delivers Israel from Balaam's cursing, Israel turns to sexual immorality with the Moabites; resulting in spiritual adultery—idolatry.	*Psalm 60:8* "Moab is my washbasin" (cf. Ps. 108:9).
1 Samuel 14:47 Saul assumes the kingship and fights against Israel's enemies, including Moab.	*Judges 10* Again, Israel runs after Moab's gods.	*Isaiah 11:14; 15; 16:2; 25:10* The prophet Isaiah condemns Moab.
2 Samuel 8:2 King David defeats the Moabites, killing two-thirds of their fighting force and forcing the rest into servitude (cf. 1 Chr. 18:2).	*1 Kings 11* King Solomon, called to lead Israel in worship of the true God, instead builds altars to Chemosh, Moab's chief deity. As was so often the case, he was led astray through his marriage to a Moabite (cf. 2 Kg. 23).	*Jeremiah 9:26; 25:21; 27:3; 48* Words of condemnation: "He who flees from the terror shall fall into the pit, and he who climbs out of the pit shall be caught in the snare. For I will bring these things upon Moab, the year of their punishment, declares the LORD."
2 Kings 3 The Moabites rebel against Israel; the Divided Kingdom is united momentarily and empowered to defeat Moab through the prophetic encouragement of Elisha.	*Nehemiah 13:23* Nehemiah discovers the post-exilic community has defiled itself by intermarrying with the Moabites.	*Ezekiel 25* "I will execute judgments upon Moab. Then they will know that I am the LORD."
2 Kings 13:20 A record of regular conflict between Israel and Moab (cf. 2 Kg. 24:2)		*Amos 2* "I will send a fire upon Moab … and Moab shall die amid uproar."
2 Chronicles 20 God miraculously delivers Jehoshaphat from the Moabite coalition through songs of praise; not a sword was needed!		*Zephaniah 2:8–9* "I have heard the taunts of Moab … how they have taunted my people.… Therefore, as I live … Moab shall become like Sodom."

Prepared by Adam T. Barr

Cast of Characters

Boaz. A member of the same clan as Naomi's husband; described as a "worthy man" or "man of valor," perhaps indicating fighting prowess and riches; provides for and eventually marries Ruth; name means "strength."

Elimelek. Naomi's husband; name means "my God is king."

Mahlon and Kilion. Sons of Elimelek and Naomi.

Naomi. Ruth's mother-in-law; adopts the name "Mara" ("bitter"); name means "beautiful."

Obed. Child of Ruth and Boaz; name means "a servant."

Orpah. A Moabite, married to Naomi's son; Ruth's sister-in-law; does not travel to Judah with Ruth and Naomi; name means "neck, skull."

Ruth. A Moabite, married to Naomi's son; travels with Naomi to Judah, a new home, new culture, and new faith; helps provide for Naomi and marries Boaz; ancestor of David and Jesus; name means "satisfied."

Chapter Overview

This curious account of an Israelite widow and her Moabite daughter-in-law highlights an emerging theme in the story of the Bible: God's saving purpose is not for Israel alone. Surely God has been particular. He called a particular man, Abraham, out of the surrounding culture to follow and obey. He called a particular nation his "firstborn son" (Ex. 4:22) and gave them his laws and ordinances to govern life and worship. But his purposes, ultimately, are much broader than the success of a single nation. God has picked this *particular* people to be heralds of his *universal* offer.

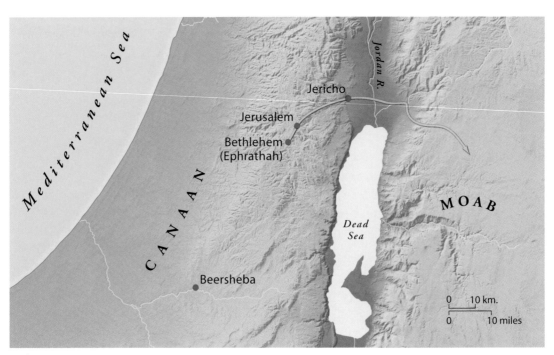

Ruth's journey.

We saw this theme already developing back in the story of Rahab, a prostitute from Jericho and an ancestor of Jesus. And here we see it once again. Ruth, a Moabite, steps out of her pagan past and into the covenant community. But there is even more to the story. This descendant of Lot's incestuous union will one day be the great-grandmother of Israel's greatest king. Like Rahab, she will stand in direct relationship to Jesus.

This snapshot of two women struggling to survive and a faithful man committed to doing the right thing is even more stunning when it is set and examined in its historical context. The events described take place during the time of the judges. The book of Judges closes with two stories, each focused on unfaithful Levites. In one a Levite lives as a prominent idol worshiper. In the second a Levite gives his concubine to be raped and murdered by fellow Israelites intent on sodomizing him. The message of these concluding stories is clear: Israel is in a bad state. And irony of ironies: a Moabite woman knows how to live for the Lord even when Israelites do not!

Section Commentary

Lost and Found (Ruth 1)

The story of Ruth opens with a curious situation: Elimelek, whose name means "my king is God," leaves his hometown, the town of Bethlehem, whose name means "house of bread" — right in the midst of a famine! The subtle message is evident: there can be no doubt that this is God's judgment for Israel's covenant-breaking idolatry. To top it off, this man, Elimelek, and his wife, Naomi, move to the land of Moab where their sons marry

Working to separate chaff from the grain.

© Franz Pagot/Alamy

Moabite women. Strictly speaking, these are the "wrong kind of girl" for a faithful Israelite man to marry.

Then, the story takes an unexpected turn: Elimelek and both of his sons die. Naomi is left alone and lost in a foreign land. Her daughter-in-law, Ruth, has just lost a husband as well. But the two women have found hope in each other. Even more, Ruth has somehow found the Lord in the process. We do not know exactly how or when this took place, but this amazing woman makes it clear that she will willingly leave her ancestral home and her gods behind her to go somewhere new with Naomi.

Making Ends Meet (Ruth 2–3)

With the death of their husbands, Naomi and Ruth were now in a vulnerable situation. Without husbands or sons, they were left open to the dangers of starvation and victimization. Ruth, especially, was particularly vulnerable as a foreigner living in Israel. Working in the fields could have made her an object for exploitation. Providentially, the Lord brought Ruth to the fields of Boaz, who took care to protect and provide for her. He instructed the field hands to allow her to glean and not to "lay a hand on" her (2:9). That phrase is drawn from a Hebrew word that could carry several meanings: "to hit, inflict injury, or have sexual relations." Boaz was determined to protect Ruth and help her make ends meet.

The Kinsman-Redeemer
(Ruth 3 – 4)

Ruth and Boaz.

In a tribal culture like Israel, family members were expected to take care of relatives. The next of kin, a male, played an especially important role in Israel, as the kinsman-redeemer, or *go'el.* He could be called upon to fulfill three specific duties:

1. To redeem property and/or relatives. In Israel, all property was a family possession, an inheritance that dated back to the time of Joshua. If land or a relative was sold to pay off debt, it was the *go'el*'s duty to pay off the debt, thereby redeeming the land or relative (Lev. 25:24 – 30, 47 – 55; Jer. 32:6 – 15).

2. To provide an heir through marriage. If a man died without an heir, it was the surviving brother's duty to marry the widow and provide an heir to carry on his brother's name and maintain his inheritance. This was called a Levirate marriage (Deut. 25:5 – 10).

3. To avenge the unlawful death of a family member. The *go'el haddam*, "avenger of blood," served a legal function in Israel, pursuing and executing justice on someone who killed a family member (Num. 35:9 – 21).

Boaz sought to fulfill this role for Ruth, not simply out of obligation, for another, closer kinsman was obligated to do that, but out of love. He had seen her faithful support of Naomi, watched her operate with integrity, and felt privileged to find such a woman.

Discussion Questions

1. As Ruth and Naomi looked back at their lives and their losses, how do you think their perspective on these things changed over time? How has your perspective on difficult life experiences changed? How has God used these experiences to lead you closer to him?

2. How does Ruth's example challenge you to grow as a faithful follower of Jesus?

3. How does Boaz serve as an Old Testament picture of Jesus Christ?

STANDING TALL, FALLING HARD

10

Plot Points

- In the case of each character in this story, we see that God is seeking people willing to trust and obey him whatever the circumstances.
- Although fathers may be faithful, this does not guarantee their children will be.
- God's people are called to covenant faithfulness, not conformity to the cultures around them.
- A leader's personality and charisma are not as important as humble obedience.

Cast of Characters

Agag. King of the Amalekites; spared by Saul though God had commanded Saul to devote all the Amalekite nation to destruction; slaughtered by Samuel; name means "roof, upper floor."

Eli. Priest of the Lord at Shiloh; mentor to Samuel; father of Hophni and Phinehas, two unworthy religious leaders; died when he learned the ark of the covenant had been stolen by the Philistines; name means "the offering, lifting up."

Elkanah. Husband of Hannah and Peninnah; father of Samuel, the last judge in Israel; appears to be a man of some prominence; name means "God the zealous" or "the zeal of God."

Hannah. Wife of Elkanah; after praying earnestly, receives a promised son; Samuel's mother; name means "gracious, merciful, one who gives."

Era of the Kings (1000–930 B.C.)

Biblical	Secular
1105 Hannah gives birth to Samuel 1050–1010 King Saul	1190 Philistines defeat Hittites and destroy capital; later defeated by Rameses III

Hophni and Phinehas. Eli's sons; priests and scoundrels; eventually killed in battle with the Philistines.

Joel and Abijah. Sons of Samuel; wicked priests.

Jonathan. Son of Saul; loyal friend of David; name means "given of God."

Kish. The son of Abiel, of the tribe of Benjamin; father of Saul, the first king of Israel; "a man of standing" from the tribe of Benjamin; name means "hard, difficult."

Nahash. King of Ammon; besieged Jabesh Gilead and offered them peace in exchange for one eye from each person in the city; army decimated Saul's army; name means "snake, serpent."

Peninnah. Elkanah's second wife; tormented Hannah over her barrenness; name means "pearl."

Samuel. A prophet and final judge of Israel; son of Elkanah and Hannah; dedicated to the Lord from before his conception; raised

David and Solomon's Kingdom.

in the temple from a young age; anointed Saul, then David, to be kings of Israel; name means "God hears," recalling he was the answer to his mother's prayers.

Saul. First king of Israel; began his rule in apparent humility and ended in madness; in between, proved again and again that human kings are no substitute for the Lord; died by his own hand in battle with the Philistines; name means "demanded."

Chapter Overview

As a small child, Samuel responded to God's call with a humble invitation: "Speak LORD, for your servant is listening" (1 Sam. 3:9–10). This simple response to God's voice is one of the touchstone moments in Scripture. It models the proper response to the call of God, a response marked by a teachable willingness to obey the direction and guidance of the Lord.

And it raises the issue of faithfulness to God yet again: "Are the Israelites listening for the voice of the Lord?" Sadly, the events of this story lead us to conclude that listening to God is likely the *last* thing on their minds. Just as they were trapped by their lust for idolatry into the worship of other gods, now they have grown envious of the political might and power of the nations around them. Since other nations have kings who provide leadership and protection, and the Israelites also want a king of their own.

At first, the Israelite experiment in kingship seems to be going well. Saul, the first king of

An Iron Age dagger in a bronze sheath from around the time of King Saul.

Israel, seems to listen for the voice of the Lord. He appears to have enough humility to recognize that he is not ready to lead God's people. His ears are wide open, and he is willing to listen when Samuel advises, but it does not take long for things to change. In a moment of pressure, Saul lends his ear to the voice of fear and disobeys a clear command from God. So much for godly leadership among God's people!

What makes Samuel, his mother before him, and the shepherd he will soon anoint so special and unique is one key characteristic: they nurture a dependency on the Lord. In this section of the story, we see Hannah pouring her heart out to God, trusting him for a child. We meet Samuel, a faithful leader and prophet, willing to respond to the Lord's direction. And, as we will soon see, David is a man after God's own heart, just as ready to break down in repentance at the Lord's convicting voice as he is to break out in celebration and worship.

As C. S. Lewis once said, each of us will either bend our knee in submission and say "Thy will be done, Lord," or we will hear God say to us on the day of judgment, "Thy will be done." The story of the first kings of Israel illustrates this fundamental choice.

Section Commentary

The Last Judge (1 Samuel 1–4)

The book of Judges describes a culture in decline, a culture in which "everyone did as they saw fit" (17:5; 21:25). This was

This relief from the main temple of Rameses III depicts the portrait of a captured Philistine.

The First King (1 Samuel 8 – 10)

Against Samuel's wishes and despite his warnings, Israel insisted on having a king so they could be like the "other nations." Samuel's warnings to the people were very specific. He warned the people that a king would do the following:

1. Take sons, making them serve with chariots and horses, in the army, in the fields and as craftsmen for the standing army. In Israel sons were a valuable part of the family structure, critical for sustaining the family economy.
2. Take daughters as perfumers, cooks, and bakers.
3. Take fields, vineyards, and olive groves and redistribute them.
4. Tax their income.
5. Freely take servants, cattle, and donkeys for his own use and as taxes.

Ultimately, Samuel concluded, the people would become slaves to the king they so desperately desired. And under the reign of Solomon's son Rehoboam, the people would finally come to see the truth in Samuel's warning.

Saul in Battle (1 Samuel 11 – 13, 15)

Much of Saul's reign as the first king of Israel was marked by war. Samuel describes several different battles, predominantly against the Philistines. But Saul also fought against Ammon and the Amalekites and in skirmishes with Moab, Edom, and Zobah. Saul won all of these early battles, except for his last battle with the Philistines. It was Saul's failure to fully destroy the Amalekites that led to his ultimate

the world into which Samuel, the thirteenth and final judge in Israel, was born. He was raised under the tutelage of Eli, a direct descendant of Aaron through the line of Ithamar. Although Eli exhibited a genuine faithfulness to the Lord (e.g., his accepting the Lord's judgment, or his response to the loss of the ark), his failure as a father caused the Lord to reject his leadership. Despite his failures as a father, Eli properly instructed Samuel in the ways of God and taught him how to hear and recognize the voice of God.

rejection as king and his downfall as a leader of God's people. Interestingly, Saul's failure to obey God would also have future consequences for the Israelites. A descendant of the spared Amalekite king, Agag, would one day threaten the entire nation of Jews with complete annihilation — Haman, the Agagite, who appears in the story of Esther centuries later.

Discussion Questions

1. How does Hannah serve as a model for trusting the Lord?

2. What do you think were some of the false beliefs that lay beneath Israel's request for a king?

3. What was Saul's chief character flaw? What, if any, steps should he have taken differently to address this?

11

FROM SHEPHERD TO KING

Plot Points

- The Lord does not look at the outward appearance but at the heart.
- Military might, represented in the giant Goliath, means nothing if you fight for the Lord.
- David, though anointed for the kingship, was willing to wait for God's perfect timing and was unwilling to dishonor God's anointed one.
- David and Jonathan's friendship presents a timeless picture of covenantal love.
- David's royal line would one day produce a Son to sit on an eternal throne.

Era of the Kings (1000–930 B.C.)

Biblical	Secular
1010–970 King David	981–942 Phoenician king Hiram I of Tyre forges alliance with Israel; David defeats and subdues the Philistines

Cast of Characters

Abinadab. A Levite who kept the ark of the covenant for twenty years; name means "father of a vow."

Abinadab. Second son of Jesse; brother of David.

Ahio. Son of Abinadab, the Levite who kept the ark for twenty years; name means "his brother."

David. Great-grandson of Boaz and Ruth; anointed second king of Israel by Samuel.

Eliab. Oldest son of Jesse; brother of David; name means "God is father."

Goliath. Philistine warrior; a giant; killed by David after challenging Israel to provide a soldier for single combat to determine the outcome of battle.

Ish-Bosheth. Youngest son of Saul; disabled by a severe fall as a young child; brought into David's household and given a favored place; name means "a man of shame."

Jesse. Grandson of Boaz and Ruth; father of David; name means "God exists."

Jonathan. Son of Saul; David's closest friend; killed in battle with the Philistines; name means "given of God."

Malki-Shua. Third son of Saul; name means "king of health."

Michal. Daughter of Saul; David's first wife; remained without children after mocking David's exuberant worship; name means "Who is perfect?"

Nathan. Prophet and adviser in Israel under David's rule; name means "given, rewarded."

Obed-Edom. Kept the ark of the covenant for three months after Uzzah was struck down by God; name means "servant of Edom."

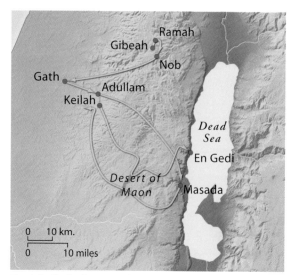

David's flight from Saul.

Samuel. Son of Elkanah and Hannah; miraculously conceived in response to Hannah's fervent prayers; raised by Eli the priest; Israel's last judge; anointed Saul as Israel's first king and David as Saul's successor; name means "God hears" or "asked of God."

Saul. Son of Kish, of the tribe of Benjamin; father of Jonathan, David's dear friend; anointed Israel's first king by Samuel; a successful military leader against the Philistines; following several acts of pride, lost the kingdom; committed suicide on the battlefield; name means "asked."

Shammah. Son of Jesse; brother of David.

Uzzah. Son of Abinadab, the Levite who kept the ark for twenty years; struck down by God when he reached out his hand to steady the ark of the covenant; name means "strength."

Chapter Overview

David's path to the throne of Israel was not easy. Although he had been called and annointed by the prophet Samuel as the true king of Israel, David would spend several years on the run, chased by the murderous, maniacal King Saul. Imagine what it would be like to be anointed by God, then forced to flee into the wilderness as an outlaw with enemies eager to destroy you! Being called by God is never a path to comfort and worldly security.

Yet David's true heart was revealed in the midst of those struggles. The same trust in the Lord that led him to fight Goliath sustained him as he camped out in caves, hiding from his enemies. Although given the chance, David chose not to strike down Saul, because he was the Lord's anointed king. David knew that the Lord himself would have to remove his enemy. A willingness to wait on the Lord defined and refined David's character. This faithful dependence upon the Lord was what finally set him apart from Saul.

We see that same patient trust when it came to building the temple. Clearly, it was a deep desire of David's heart. On one hand, it would have been very easy to move forward with the project because he had the means, and it was a worthy goal. Then why not proceed? Simply put, because the Lord said, "Wait," and David did so.

The image of David dancing before the ark with wild abandon, uninhibited and unconcerned with his reputation, produces a sharp contrast to the pictures that many have of

This Assyrian carving shows the type of slingshot David likely used to kill Goliath.

what a king's behavior should be. David trusted the Lord and gave himself wholly to him. Waiting for the kingship, or the temple, or anything else the Lord might have was all right with David, because he knew the Lord would provide the best.

Section Commentary

The Lord's Anointed
(1 Samuel 16)

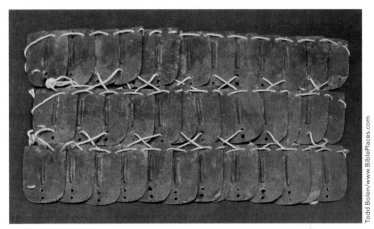

Bronze armor scales from the 9th-7th century B.C.

We say, "Don't judge a book by its cover," but how often do we follow our own advice? In reality, humans have an innate reflex for making assumptions at first glance. Samuel did it as he viewed Jesse's sons. He judged based on outward appearance.

But the Lord was looking at an individual's heart that day and saw someone who would care more about doing the Lord's will than pleasing others or himself. One thousand years later, a descendant of David, Jesus of Nazareth, would also be anointed, this time by the Holy Spirit in the Jordan River. He, too, was someone you might pass over at first glance, but his heart was perfectly aligned with the will of his Father in heaven. He, like his ancestor David, was also a man after God's own heart.

David and Goliath (1 Samuel 17)

Goliath was an unbelievably imposing figure, standing over nine feet tall. The Bible makes reference to other examples of giants (e.g., the Nephilim [Gen. 6:4; Num. 13:33], Anakim, and Rephaim), but Goliath is displayed in full 3-D in this passage. He not only stands tall but is wearing the best armor. Scripture describes it in detail. Based on archaeological studies, for his day Goliath had "the best of the best" military hardware. Not only that, but Goliath knew how to use his equipment, having been raised in the company of warriors from his youth. In every way, he was poised to crush David like a gnat.

One-on-one combat was celebrated in ancient literature as a way to see whose god was strongest. Examples can be found in Greek, Egyptian, and Hittite literature. Clearly, David knew that size and skill were not the deal breakers. The real question was who had the Lord on his side.

David and Jonathan (1 Samuel 18)

David and Jonathan's friendship was powerful and unique. The exchange of weapons described in this passage certainly indicated a deep commitment to each other. But Jonathan's act of giving his robe to David may have represented more than a sign of close friendship.

In other ancient texts, we learn that laying down one's robe could have legal implications. For instance, a son expelled from his father's household would lay his robe on a stool near the door. This symbolized his relinquishing any claim to the family inheritance. Another ancient text describes a prince who chooses to leave his throne. He lays his mantle on the throne, indicating the legal relinquishment of the throne (cf. V. Philips Long, *1 Samuel*, in ZIBBC, 353).

David and Saul
(1 Samuel 18, 24; Psalm 59)

Saul's madness and David's innocence lie at the narrative core of the Saul-David conflict. In Saul we see a man desperately trying to preserve what he knows is already lost. In David we see a hero all the more admirable for his unwillingness to grab power under the wrong circumstances (i.e., after killing the "Lord's anointed").

A Tragic End (1 Samuel 31; 2 Samuel 22)

If Saul had been taken alive, he most likely would have faced a gruesome death. In the ancient world, it was common for prisoners, particularly important prisoners, to undergo a slow, painful execution. Assyrian reliefs make that evident, sometimes depicting people impaled on stakes or even being skinned alive.

The passing of Saul was a tragic end for one with such potential early in his reign. The passing of Jonathan was a tragic loss of friendship for David.

Unashamed (2 Samuel 6)

Once again we see how David was a man after God's own heart. He placed personal dignity aside and danced with everything he had. This moment illustrates the difference between Saul and David. Saul was always concerned with how he would be perceived by other people. David was not. He danced before an audience of one, even as others watched on in contempt.

A House for the Lord (1 Chronicles 17)

David expressed a deep longing to provide a house for the Lord. Although his desires were affirmed, the Lord made it clear: "This project is for your son" (see 1 Kings 5:5). However, the Lord promised even more to David, saying: "I will build *your* house" (see 2 Sam. 7:27). In this passage we see one of the clearest expressions of God's plan to bring his Son's eternal throne to earth.

Discussion Questions

1. What does David's story teach us about the importance of not only knowing *what* God wants, but *how* God would have us bring it to pass?

2. How does the friendship of David and Jonathan inspire you to seek deeper friendship?

3. How does David's exuberant worship challenge the "temperature" of your worship?

4. Looking back through the lens of Jesus Christ, how do you read God's promise to build David's household? How do you think David understood this promise?

THE TRIALS OF A KING

12

Plot Points

- Not even a king is above the law, and what is done in secret will one day be revealed.
- When called out for our sin, the only proper response is honest repentance.
- Our sins can be forgiven, but that does not mean the consequences will be erased.

Cast of Characters

Abishai. Son of Zeruiah, David's sister; helped command David's army; name means "the present of my father."

Absalom. Third son of David and Maachah; tried to remove and replace his father as king; killed by Joab; name means "father of peace."

Bathsheba. Wife of Uriah the Hittite; married David and gave birth to Solomon; an ancestor of Jesus; name means "the seventh daughter."

Ittai. A commander in David's army.

Jedidiah. A name given to Solomon by Nathan; means "beloved of the Lord."

Jehiel. Helped collect and safeguard treasures given for the building of the temple.

Joab. Son of Zeruiah, David's sister; commander in David's army; helped cover up David's adulterous relationship with Bathsheba, the wife of Uriah; killed David's son Absalom; name means "paternity."

Era of the Kings (1000–930 B.C.)

Biblical	Secular
1010–970 King David	1100–1000 Assyrians rising to power
	1069–945 Egyptian Dynasty XXI
	1012–972 Ashur-rabi II, king of Assyria

Nathan. Prophet and adviser in Israel under David's rule; called David to account for his adultery with Bathsheba; name means "given, rewarded."

Solomon. Son of David and Bathsheba; fol-lowed David as king; name means "peaceable, perfect, one who recompenses."

Uriah. A Hittite; husband of Bathsheba; a soldier in David's army murdered by David's order to cover up David's adultery.

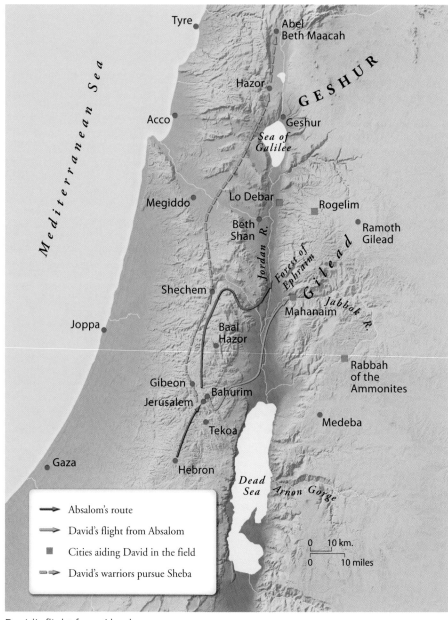

David's flight from Absalom.

Chapter Overview

The story is tragic. For one moment of pleasure, David compromises everything. He loses his integrity, and he leaves broken lives in his wake. Although the Lord granted him forgiveness, David lived with the consequences of his sin for the rest of his reign.

The story of Absalom is not simply the story of a power-hungry son. It is the story of David's chickens coming home to roost. Nathan had told David, "What you did in secret will be done to you in broad daylight." David had stolen another man's wife and tried to cover it up. Absalom, on the rooftop of the palace in full view of the people, took David's concubines.

The problems in David's family began even before Absalom's rebellion. Another of David's sons actually raped his own half sister. David did nothing to address the injustice, very likely because he felt he was in no position to occupy the moral high ground. David's moral compromise with Bathsheba had left him open and vulnerable to criticism. His son Absalom saw the injustice against his sister and nurtured his hatred for two full years before killing that brother. Soon afterward, his resentment against his father led to open rebellion.

As we see in this section, David's sin with Bathsheba had ripple effects. Although he was forgiven, the consequences of his moral failure lived on. In every story we have read so far, we have seen that there is no such thing as a *perfect* person. In the end, each of the heroes in Scripture does something to perpetuate the brokenness ushered in by Adam and Eve.

Section Commentary

David and Bathsheba
(2 Samuel 11)

The spring was the traditional time for military campaigns in the ancient Near East. By that time the rains of winter had ceased, and harvest had not yet arrived. David's first mistake was his decision not to lead his men out to battle. He was in the wrong place at the

David and Bathsheba.

Absalom's tomb (tall, pointed structure) is located in the Kidron Valley outside Jerusalem.

wrong time, home alone when he should have been out protecting his people from invading armies.

The flat-roof structure of that day explains how David was able to walk on the roof. Bathsheba was likely engaged in purification rites following menstruation. Why she would bathe in a place that could expose her to public view, we are not told. Whether Bathsheba bore some level of culpability is not the focus of the narrator. Rather, he focuses on David's failure as a man and king.

Conviction and Repentance
(2 Samuel 12; Psalm 51)

David immediately repents when confronted by Nathan. Although he had been caught up in a web of deception and murder, when called out, he did not hide. This alone indicates what an exceptional figure David was.

Consequences (2 Samuel 12; Psalm 32)

Nathan outlines two consequences for David's sin. First, that the child they have conceived will die. Second, that what David did to Uriah in secret will be done to him publicly by someone whom he trusts. That someone turned out to be his son, Absalom.

Absalom (2 Samuel 18 – 19)

Absalom seems to have been driven by more than mere ambition. His sister Tamar was raped by their half brother Amnon. Tamar came to live with Absalom after this happened, and he saw how disgraced and desolated she was by the event. He also saw that David, though angry, did nothing to Amnon. Absalom waited two years then struck, killing his half brother. Clearly, he had harbored rage in his heart. Some of this, no doubt, drove his rebellion.

Solomon (1 Chronicles 22, 29)

David groomed Solomon to follow him to the throne. He included Solomon in the planning for the temple, passing on a passion for the project. In addition to gathering the workforce and supplies he would need, David surrounded Solomon with trusted counselors.

The Shepherd
(Psalm 23)

In the ancient Near East, the metaphor of shepherd could apply to both kings and gods. One Sumerian text provides an example of the latter: "A man's personal god is a shepherd who finds pasturage for him. Let him lead him like a sheep to the grass they can eat" (J. W. Hilber, *Psalms*, in ZIBBC, ed. J. H. Walton, 342).

Discussion Questions

1. David appears to have developed a sense of privileged exceptionalism, saying, "I deserve this." How can that attitude infect us? Give some examples.

2. Describe the steps David took that led him from lust to murder. Discuss these steps in light of James 1:13 – 15.

3. What were the consequences of David's cover-up? Have you ever experienced heartfelt repentance yet still had to live with consequences? Explain.

13 THE KING WHO HAD IT ALL

Plot Points

- The temple is completed and filled with the glory of God.
- Solomon's wisdom was a gift from God. Israel prospered and grew in reputation through Solomon's leadership.
- Solomon's many foreign wives were a snare, leading him into idolatry, costing him the kingdom.

Cast of Characters

Abishag. A beautiful Shunammite woman who attended David in his old age.

Asaph, Heman, Jeduthun. Levite musicians; played at the consecration of the temple.

Bathsheba. Wife of David; mother of Solomon.

Hiram. King of Tyre.

Pharaoh. Probably Siamun, pharaoh during the Twenty-first Dynasty.

Queen of Sheba. Probably from the region near Yemen, at the western edge of Arabia; oversaw a tribal kingdom.

Solomon. Son of David and Bathsheba; followed David as king; responsible for building Israel's first temple; writer of many proverbs, poems, and philosophical reflections; acquired great power and wealth; ultimately led astray by his many wives.

Era of the Kings (1000–930 B.C.)

Biblical	Secular
970–930 King Solomon	972–967 Ashur-resh-ishi III, king of Assyria 945–924 Pharaoh Sheshonq I 940–915 Hezion (Rezon), king of Syria

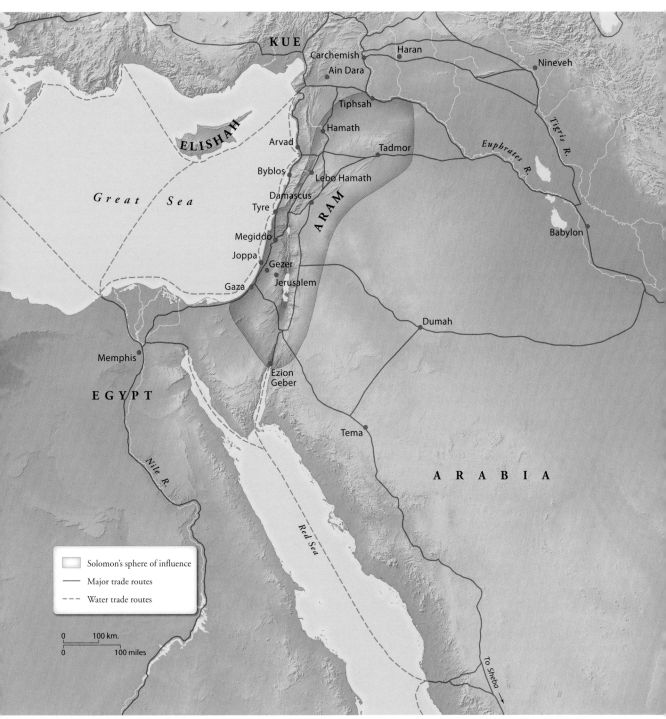

KUE

Carchemish
Haran
Nineveh
Ain Dara

Tiphsah

ELISHAH

Hamath
Arvad

Tadmor

Euphrates R.

Tigris R.

Byblos
Lebo Hamath

Great Sea

Damascus
ARAM
Tyre

Babylon

Megiddo
Joppa
Gezer
Gaza
Jerusalem

Dumah

Memphis

Ezion
Geber

EGYPT

Tema

Nile R.

ARABIA

Red Sea

To Sheba

Solomon's sphere of influence

Major trade routes

Water trade routes

0   100 km.
0   100 miles

Solomon's kingdom. To fund his vast building projects and standing army, Solomon divided Israel into twelve districts, each led by a governor who collected taxes and provided material support to Solomon.

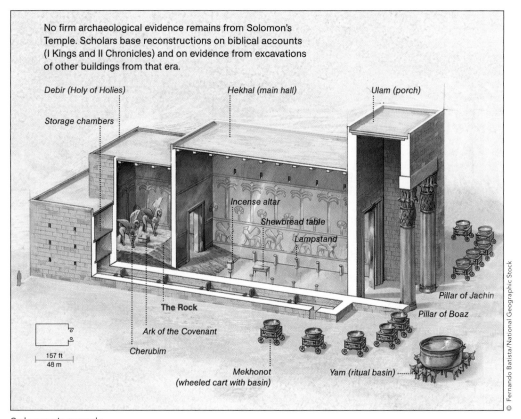

No firm archaeological evidence remains from Solomon's Temple. Scholars base reconstructions on biblical accounts (I Kings and II Chronicles) and on evidence from excavations of other buildings from that era.

Debir (Holy of Holies)

Storage chambers

Hekhal (main hall)

Ulam (porch)

Incense altar

Shewbread table

Lampstand

The Rock

Pillar of Jachin

Pillar of Boaz

Ark of the Covenant

Cherubim

157 ft
48 m

Mekhonot
(wheeled cart with basin)

Yam (ritual basin)

© Fernando Batista/National Geographic Stock

Solomon's temple.

Chapter Overview

If David was a warrior, Solomon was a builder. If David cleared the ground, Solomon filled it. Solomon built buildings. He took the treasures David had collected and formed them into a glorious temple. He built himself a grand palace. He built stables for his many horses and chariots. He built storehouses for his vast wealth.

Solomon also built alliances. His first marriage was to the daughter of a pharaoh. His many other wives, in one way or another, strengthened his ties to surrounding nations. He built a bureaucratic system, dividing Israel into twelve districts and imposing taxes to fund his many programs. Solomon built a body of intellectual work. He authored proverbs, love poems, and great works of philosophy. He sat in judgment and decided cases with such wisdom as to become legend.

But Solomon also built altars to foreign gods. He built a harem and family of wives that led him to sacrifice on those altars. Even as he was building structures and systems that could strengthen his kingdom, he was building practices that would destroy it.

When Samuel warned the people against choosing a king, he had someone like Solomon in mind. Why? Because Solomon built his many accomplishments on the backs of the Israelites. Even as he was erecting what seemed like timeless monuments, Solomon was eroding the foundation of any stable monarchy. Although he would not have to deal with the people's bitterness, his son would, and it would divide the kingdom. Solomon was a builder, but his building came at a great cost — the eventual breaking of the nation.

Section Commentary

Except That ... (1 Kings 1–3)

At the very beginning of Solomon's story, we read that he "showed his love for the LORD by walking according to the instructions given him by his father David, except that..." (3:3). Solomon's talent, wisdom, and leadership were all undoubtedly exceptional. We even see a genuine desire to please God. However, it was the "except thats" in his life that ultimately defined him.

No Equal (1 Kings 3–4)

Throughout his proverbs, Solomon extols the treasure of wisdom. It is more precious than gold or jewels. Perhaps no other person in history has occupied such a position to speak of the benefits of wisdom more than Solomon. When he asked for wisdom above all things, the Lord promised he would have "no equal among kings." That request would overflow into wise governance and great wealth.

Proverbs (Proverbs 1–3, 6, 20, 21)

H. H. Halley defined a proverb as "a Short, Pithy, Axiomatic Saying ... Designed primarily for the Young: a form of Teaching: repetition of Practical Thoughts in form that would stick in mind." Solomon's proverbs represent an

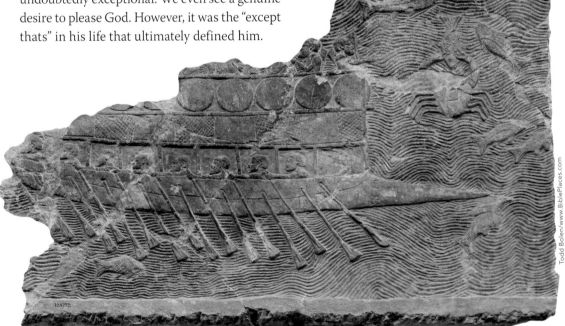

Todd Bolen/www.BiblePlaces.com

A relief of a Phoenician warship used by Assyrians, 700 B.C. Similar ships may have been used during Solomon's reign.

effort to insert the law of God into all of life. It is a demonstration of wisdom (i.e., knowledge rightly applied), for the one presenting the proverbs has actually lived, tested, and seen the fruit of his words.

The Temple Formed and Filled
(1 Kings 5 – 8; 2 Chronicles 5 – 7)

The Old Testament is filled with the motif of God's presence with humans. It begins in the garden of Eden and moves through the accounts of Abraham and Moses. Here again we see God's intention to make his home with humanity. The building and filling of the temple with the presence of God is a foreshadowing of the incarnation, when the Son of God became a man and God himself walked among us (see John 1:14). It also hints at the nature of the church, our identity as a living temple filled with the presence of God's Spirit (see 1 Pet. 2:5). Finally, it points us to the hope and the promise of the new heavens and new earth, when God will finally make his dwelling with his people, forever (see Rev. 21:3).

Accumulation (1 Kings 10 – 11)

Jesus said that it is easier for a camel to go through the eye of a needle than for a rich man to enter the kingdom of God. Wealth itself is not condemnable, but it all too often allows character weaknesses to be explored and exploited. Solomon's great wealth opened the door for him to travel many avenues. Eventually he lost his way and was corrupted by his great wealth.

Discussion Questions

1. Make a list of the things Solomon "got right." From this list, pick and discuss one or two that personally challenge and/or inspire you.

2. Make a list of the things Solomon "got wrong." From this list, pick and discuss one or two that personally convict and/or serve as helpful warnings for you.

3. How can accumulating "stuff" become a danger to one's spiritual life? How does life in our world make that danger even more acute?

A KINGDOM TORN IN TWO

14

Plot Points

- In three generations, Israel came to see that Samuel's warnings about monarchy were true.
- Following Solomon's rule, the divided kingdoms were marked by unfaithfulness to the Lord and nationalized idolatry, with righteous kings being the exception.
- Only the Lord's continuing regard for the house of David kept his hand of judgment from falling.

The Divided Kingdom

Judah (930–586 b.c.)	Israel (930–722 b.c.)
930–913 King Rehoboam	930–909 King Jeroboam I
872–848 King Jehoshaphat	875–848 Elijah
740–681 Isaiah	874–853 King Ahab
715–686 King Hezekiah	848–797 Elisha
697–642 King Manasseh	760–750 Amos
640–609 King Josiah	750–715 Hosea
626–585 Jeremiah	722 Fall of the northern kingdom
609–598 King Jehoiakim	
605–530 Daniel	
597–586 King Zedekiah	
593–571 Ezekiel	
586 Fall of Jerusalem	

Cast of Characters

Abijah. Son of Jeroboam, king of Israel; died in his youth; name means "the Lord is my father."

Abijah. Son of Rehoboam; second king of Judah; ruled three years; name means "the Lord is my father"; did evil.

Adoniram. In charge of forced labor under David, Solomon, and Rehoboam; stoned to death by the people; name means "Lord is most high."

Ahab. Son of Omri; seventh king of Israel; married to Jezebel, daughter of a foreign king and idolater; name means "uncle"; did evil.

Ahijah. A prophet from Shiloh; prophesied the split of the kingdom; name means "brother of the Lord."

Asa. Son of Abijah; third king of Judah; a righteous king whose heart "was fully committed to the LORD all his life" (1 Kings 15:14; 2 Chron. 15:17); name means "physician."

Baasha. Assassinated Jeroboam and his entire family; third king of Israel; waged constant war with Asa, king of Judah; name means "he who seeks or lays waste"; did evil before the Lord.

Ben-Hadad. Son of Tabrimmon; king of Aram, ruling in Damascus; made treaty with Asa; name means "son of Hadad."

Hiel of Bethel. Rebuilt Jericho at the cost of his sons Abiram and Segub, as prophesied by Joshua; name means "God lives."

Jehoshaphat. Son of Asa; fourth king of Judah; name means "the Lord is judge"; did right before the Lord.

Jeroboam. First king of the divided northern kingdom of Israel; rebelled against Rehoboam, Solomon's son and successor; erected golden statues to replace temple worship; ruled twenty-one years; name means "he who opposes the people"; did evil before the Lord.

Jezebel. Wife of Ahab; daughter of Ethbaal, king of Sidon; worshiper of Baal and Asherah; name means "chaste."

Josiah. Prophesied descendant of David; sixteenth king of Judah; ruled when the Book of the Law was discovered; name means "the Lord burns"; did right before the Lord.

Maakah. Daughter of Abishalom; wife of Rehoboam; mother of Abijah.

Naamah. Wife of Solomon; mother of Rehoboam, an Ammonite; name means "beautiful."

Nadab. Son of Jeroboam; did "evil in the eyes of the LORD, following the ways of his father" (1 Kings 15:26); name means "free and voluntary gift, prince."

Omri. Father of Ahab; sixth king of Israel; made Samaria the capital of the northern kingdom; name means "sheaf of corn"; did evil before the Lord.

Rehoboam. Son of Solomon; first king of Judah; continued and hardened his father's harshest policies; name means "who sets the people at liberty"; did evil before the Lord.

Shemaiah. A prophet who warned Rehoboam not to pursue war; name means "that hears or obeys the Lord."

Shishak. Alternate name of Shoshenq I, an Egyptian pharaoh; attacked Jerusalem and plundered the temple under Rehoboam's rule.

Zimri. Assassinated Elah to win the throne of Israel; committed suicide after seven days on the throne; name means "my field, my vine."

Chapter Overview

Just three generations before Rehoboam, Israel had begged for a king. They believed that having a king would unite the separate tribes and form one strong nation. They dreamed they could be just like the nations around them, with a national identity centered around a royal line. But by the time Rehoboam

The Black Obelisk shows Israel's King Jehu bowing before Shalmaneser III.

assumed the throne, the dream of past generations had become a nightmare.

The monarchy, from this point forward, would be one of the key sources of the nation's undoing. When Rehoboam tried to carry on his father's forced labor policies, rebellion erupted. Jeroboam, a prophesied leader with great potential, would only lead the people deeper into idolatry in a futile effort to shore up his own power base.

Six in twenty kings of Judah would be categorized as "doing right" in the Lord's eyes. Israel was even worse, with only one king, Jehu, rising to the level of a "mixed" record. As went the monarchy, so went the nation. Rather than strengthening Israel and uniting them as one, the monarchy became the catalyst for the eventual dissolution of the nation.

Section Commentary

The Split (1 Kings 12)

Rehoboam exhibited all the shortcomings of arrogant youth. He rejected the advice of older, wiser men. He put his trust entirely in his peers, and he failed to listen to his people's concern. Most importantly, he did not diagnose the fractures that had risen between the monarchy and the populace. Under his father's rule, heavy burdens had been laid on the people. He

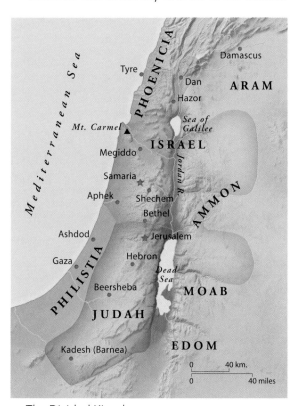

The Divided Kingdom.

did not realize that the people were just waiting for an excuse to anoint Jeroboam and set up a rival to the throne!

Calves . . . Again (1 Kings 12 – 14)

Like King Saul, Jeroboam did not understand that he was not ultimately responsible for maintaining the loyalty of the people. If he was willing to be a man after God's own heart, then the people would follow, as they had with David. But, as Saul did when he offered sacrifice without Samuel, Jeroboam wanted to seal the people to himself. And so the golden calf idols rose again as the hearts of God's people were seduced and trapped by foreign gods and the worship of idols.

An Inheritance Plundered
(1 Kings 14 – 16)

In the desert Moses had received an overwhelming collection of treasure from the people for the building of the tabernacle. When David began preparing for the temple, he too saw the people bring their best gifts for the Lord's dwelling place. Who would have known that his grandson would see that great treasure plundered by an invading force!

A bull that is a gilded bronze votive offering ("the golden calf"), from the temple of Baalat-Gebal in Byblos, Lebanon.

Sadly it was more than gold and silver that was being plundered and lost. David's descendants had been "robbed" of their greatest inheritance, the Lord and his law! By the time of King Josiah, the Book of the Law, which Joshua had told the people to treasure, had been lost to the point that it had to be "rediscovered" in a dusty storeroom of the temple. Israel's greatest treasure had been hidden away, and the nation would reap the consequences of that mistake for generations to come.

Discussion Questions

1. How did the rule of Solomon affect his son, Rehoboam?

2. What motivated Jeroboam to erect the golden calf idols? What does this tell us about Jeroboam's trust in God?

3. What are the key similarities and differences between the time of the judges and the time of the kings?

GOD'S MESSENGERS

15

Plot Points

- Under the leadership of Ahab and Jezebel, Israel is gripped by idolatry and greed.
- God sends prophets to call Israel to repent, but they are largely ignored.
- The power of God wins every time!

Cast of Characters

Ahab. Son of Omri; seventh king of Israel; married to Jezebel, daughter of a foreign king and idolater; name means "uncle"; killed in battle while wearing a disguise; an evil king.

Amos. A prophet in Israel during the reigns of Uzziah and Jeroboam; shepherd from Tekoa; name means "loading, weighty."

Ben-Hadad. King of Aram, a powerful force in the ancient Near East at that time.

Elijah. A prophet of the Lord; from Tishbe in Gilead; prophesied in Israel against Ahab and Jezebel and their prophets; taken to heaven in a chariot of fire; name means "God the Lord."

Elisha. Disciple of Elijah and his successor; from Abel Meholah; name means "salvation of God."

Assyrian Rule

Israel (930–722 B.C.)	Assyrian Resurgence (1076–750)
930–909 King Jeroboam I	883–859 Ashurnasirpal I expands south and west, collecting tribute and plundering
875–848 Elijah	859–823 Shalmaneser III establishes control over Israel
874–853 King Ahab	**Neo-Assyrian Period (750–625)**
848–797 Elisha	
760–750 Amos	745–727 Tiglath-pileser III
750–715 Hosea	727–722 Shalmaneser V defeats Samaria
722 Fall of the northern kingdom	

Gehazi. Servant of Elisha; struck with leprosy for seeking payment when Elisha healed Naaman, a commander of the armies of Aram; name means "valley of sight."

Hazael. Anointed king of Aram by Elijah.

Hosea. A prophet in Israel; preached a message of repentance; name means "savior."

Jehoahaz. Son of Jehu; eleventh king of Israel; lost Israel's army; an evil king.

Jehoash. Son of Jehoahaz; twelfth king of Israel; name means "fire of the Lord"; an evil king.

Jehu. Anointed by Elijah; tenth king of Israel; purged Israel of pagan altars; name means "himself who exists"; had a mixed record.

Jeroboam II. Thirteenth king of Israel; improved Israel's security but not their fidelity to the Lord; name means "he who opposes the people."

Jezebel. Wife of Ahab; worshiper of Baal and Asherah; tried to kill Elijah; thrown from a balcony to her death and consumed by dogs according to prophecy.

Naboth. Murdered by King Ahab for his vineyard; name means "words."

Prophets of Asherah. Official advisers to Jezebel; exposed as frauds by Elijah and slaughtered in Kishon Valley.

Prophets of Baal. Official advisers to Jezebel; exposed as frauds by Elijah and slaughtered in Kishon Valley.

The ministries of Elijah and Elisha.

Chapter Overview

The northern kingdom, Israel, had suffered under six evil kings. Jeroboam started them off on the wrong foot, erecting golden calf idols to replace temple worship. But each king after him had done his best to make things worse. Tragically, the people were going along for the ride. Archaeological evidence paints a troubling picture: Even as the Israelites ran from the Lord, they were experiencing amazing prosperity. People lived in vast homes and drank expensive wine. For those living in Israel, things felt just fine. Life was good, and few worried about the consequences of their idolatry and the abandonment of God's law.

In reality, however, Israel was on the brink of destruction. The Lord had withheld his judgment for a time to allow the people an opportunity to repent, but he could not allow their rebellion and sin to continue. Nevertheless, before the ax would finally fall, God gave his people several warnings through his prophets.

Elijah came with the message that Baal and Asherah were no match for the Lord. Baal, with all his supposed power over the storm, could not open the heavens if the Lord had closed them. Elisha demonstrated that the Lord alone could bring healing, not sorcerers who sold their charms. Amos was even more straightforward, providing detailed descriptions of the pain that was approaching if Israel did not turn away from idolatry.

Hosea had one of the most distinctive prophetic ministries in the Old Testament. Many prophets would dramatically embody their message by wearing sackcloth or buying a field in the middle of a siege. But Hosea was instructed to marry a woman who was continuously unfaithful and prostituted herself. His faithfulness to his adulterous wife was a real-life portrayal of God's faithful, covenantal love for his people.

The prophets God sent to his adulterous people brought a message that cut. Their words often carried a stinging rebuke and warnings of impending judgment and doom. But they were also a message offering a way out — a word of hope and salvation. The problem then, as it still is today, is that many people would rather have their feelings stroked and their selfish comforts satisfied than their souls saved!

Section Commentary

The Fire of the Lord and the Wrath of a Queen
(1 Kings 17 – 19)

A Phoenician seal of Jezebel.
Z. Radovan/www.BibleLandPictures.com

There are moments in the story of Scripture when God wins a battle with a touch of the dramatic. It happened with David when he faced Goliath — the untrained youth taking on the seasoned warrior and winning the fight through faith in God. Now, we witness yet another dramatic confrontation with Elijah and the priests of Jezebel.

Elijah stands as an outsider in this situation. He is facing off against the powerful religious and political figures who control the heart of the nation of Israel. These were the official advisers to the queen. And Elijah was ... no one, really.

Still, Elijah courageously confronted King Ahab and Queen Jezebel by directly challenging the prests of Baal and Asherah. The king and queen had normalized Baal worship in Israel, making Israel a more mainstream player in Near Eastern politics. Their commitment to Baal was more than a religious one; it was a social statement that Israel was "at the table" with all its neighbors. Elijah was not only challenging their idolatry, he was criticizing their governing strategy and actively working against their ambitious plan to make Israel a player in international politics.

More fundamentally, though, Elijah was calling the nation of Israel to turn it's heart back to the Lord. Elijah was shocked that the people had once again given themselves to a false god. He stood amazed that they would revere and rely on a "god" who was nothing more than stone and wood. And he was horrified that they would devote themselves to a power that required them to sacrifice their own children. The showdown between Elijah and the false priests of Baal was really an opportunity to remind Israel that there was only one, true God. And his name wasn't Baal or Asherah.

Fresh Fire (1 Kings 19)

Following his great victory over the priests of Baal, Elijah was cast into a deep depression. His suffering was more than just a fear of Jezebel, who had threatened his life. He poured out his frustration and sadness to the Lord: "The Israelites have rejected your covenant, torn down your altars, and put your prophets to death with the sword. I am the only one left, and now they are trying to kill me too" (v. 14).

Elijah's grief stemmed from more than fear for his own safety. After all, he had already indicated his willingness to take risks and face down dangerous situations. He was saddened because from his limited perspective, he alone remained to remember the covenant in all of Israel. Elijah grew depressed and discouraged because he felt alone. The Lord, however, provided Elijah with a reminder of the truth: that there were others besides Elijah who carried the vision and remembered the Lord and his covenant. In fact, God was about to go one step further. He would grant Elijah a partner and a successor to his ministry.

Chariots of Fire (2 Kings 2)

Overfamiliarity with this story causes us to miss at least two thematically rich elements. First, we take for granted the fact that Elijah is taken "up" into heaven. After centuries of Christian tradition, the concept of rising "up" to be with God in heaven is nothing new to us. To the Israelite mind, however, this was a great and unique honor being afforded to Elijah. In the ancient world, people were entombed in the earth and buried to rest with their ancestors, not lifted up into the heavens. Second, in

An infant burial jar from Ashkelon. Children were often sacrificed to pagan gods.

Joshua Walton, courtesy of the Leon Levy Expedition to Ashkelon

Erich Lessing/Art Resource, NY

A prisoner being led away by a nose ring. Prisoners were usually made into slaves to serve their captors.

the ancient Near East, the god Baal was known as "the Charioteer," often portrayed with the storm clouds as his war chariot. Like much of his ministry, Elijah's ascension to heaven was yet another statement against the false religion of his day: the Lord, not Baal, is God!

God at Work through Elisha
(2 Kings 4, 6)

It is interesting to compare Elijah and Elisha's ministries. Elijah's was confrontational, a wild-eyed, in-your-face stand against the idolatry of Ahab and Jezebel. Many of his miracles were "nature miracles" — drought, fire from heaven, and miraculous rainfall. On the other hand, Elisha's ministry was primarily defined by

miracles of compassion. Consider the list: the purification of the water at Jericho; the miraculous supply of oil for the widow; the miraculous birth of a son and his resurrection from the dead; the poisoned pot; the multiplied loaves; the healing of Naaman's leprosy; the ax head floating; the blinding, capturing, feeding, and releasing of the soldiers of Aram; the routing of Syria's armies and salvation of Samaria. The God of Elijah and Elisha not only commands the forces of nature, he is powerful enough to bring healing and help to his people in need.

The Shepherd of Tekoa
(Amos 1, 3 – 5, 9)

Samaria, the capital of the northern kingdom, stood on a three-hundred-foot hill overlooking a beautiful valley. Samaria was like a jewel in the mountains. Within the city, but especially in the outlying hill country, archaeologists have found evidence of great wealth. Squarely in Amos's crosshairs are those wealthy Israelites who have built mansions for themselves on the backs of the poor: "'They do not know how to do right,' declares the LORD, 'who store up in their fortresses what they have plundered and looted'" (3:10).

Fire on Their Cities
(Hosea 4 – 5, 8 – 9, 14)

Hosea likens the Lord's judgment to a fire that will fall on their cities. When left unattended, fire can spread through a forest. It might start small, but if it is allowed to run wild, the damage can be devastating. Hosea warned Israel, "Put out the fire now!" Sadly, they failed to heed his warning, and the fires of judgment would eventually burn hot with God's anger toward the sin of his people.

Discussion Questions

1. The prophets must have struggled greatly to keep ministering despite feeling that their efforts were not changing anything. How are we called to give witness in our culture, regardless of whether we can see the effects of our labor?

2. Hosea wrote, "A spirit of prostitution is in their heart; they do not acknowledge the LORD.... They are unfaithful to the LORD; they give birth to illegitimate children" (5:4, 7). What do you think he was getting at? How do you think this could be applied to us?

THE BEGINNING OF THE END
(of the Kingdom of Israel)

16

Plot Points

- At last, God's patience with Israel is spent, and the northern kingdom falls to the Assyrian Empire, never to rise again.
- Judah illustrates what happens when God's people allow him to be their ally. Even the mightiest empires fall back before him!
- In Isaiah's prophecy, we see the clearest witness to the coming Messiah.

Cast of Characters

Ahaz. Thirteenth king of Judah; known for disastrous religious, military, and diplomatic ventures.

Eliakim. Son of Hilkiah; palace administrator under Hezekiah; name means "resurrection of God."

Esarhaddon. Son of Sennacherib, succeeded him as king; one of the greatest kings of Assyria.

Hezekiah. Twelfth king of Judah; stood strong in faith against the armies of Assyria and its supreme commander; name means "strength of the Lord."

Hoshea. Son of Elah; king of Israel in Samaria; betrayed his alliance with Assyria, turning to Egypt; captured and imprisoned by Shalmaneser; did evil in the Lord's eyes; name means "deliverer."

The Kingdom of Israel

Israel (930–722 B.C.)	Neo-Assyrian Period (750–625)
746 6 months **Zechariah**, 14th king of Israel	745–727 **Tiglath-pileser III**
746 1 month **Shallum**, 15th king of Israel	• Consolidated control over Syria
746–737 **Menahem**, 16th king of Israel	• Campaigned to subdue Syro-Ephraimite coalition
736–735 **Pekahiah**, 17th king of Israel	727–722 **Shalmaneser V**
734–731 **Pekah**, 18th king of Israel	• Captured Shechem
730–723 **Hoshea**, last king of Israel	• Besieged Tyre
722 Fall of the northern kingdom	• Defeated Samaria

Isaiah. Major prophet to Judah for more than sixty years; began prophetic calling under Uzziah, king of Judah, and ministered eight years into the reign of Manasseh; gave detailed prophecies of the coming Messiah; spoke out against Israel's idolatry; called the "prince of the prophets"; name means "salvation of God."

Joah. Son of Asaph; recorder under Hezekiah.

Sargon II. King of Assyria; deported twenty-seven thousand people from Israel.

Sennacherib. King of Assyria; attempted to intimidate Hezekiah; blasphemed the Lord, "daring" Hezekiah to rely on God; assassinated by his own sons, Adrammelek and Sharezer, while worshiping his god Nisrok.

Shalmaneser. King of Assyria; attacked Israel and deported a large number of Israelites in 721 B.C.

Shebna. Secretary under Hezekiah.

So. Egyptian pharaoh; may be an abbreviated form of Osorkon IV, last pharaoh of the Twenty-second Dynasty, or Tefnakht, pharaoh of an overlapping Twenty-fourth Dynasty located in Sais.

Tirhakah. King of Cush.

Uzziah. Also called Azariah; king of Judah; struck by leprosy while performing the duties of a priest; reigned fifty-two years; name means "the Lord has helped."

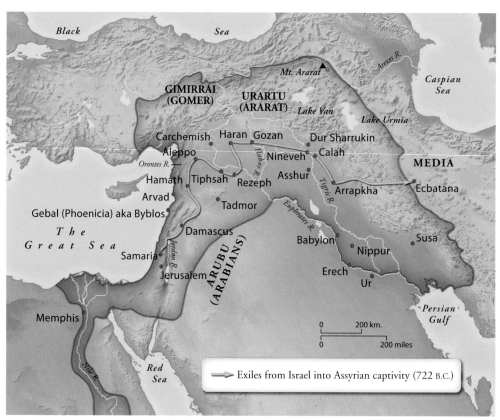

The exile of Israel.

Chapter Overview

Israel lived in the midst of massive empires. To the southwest, mighty Egypt had stood for over a millennium. To the southeast, Babylon was on the rise as a world power. To the northeast, Assyria ruled as the biggest bully on the block. For a smaller nation like Israel, the "logical" way to survive, surrounded by bullies, was to make strategic alliances. Hoshea, the last king of Israel, must have figured, "If one alliance is good, two must be even better." When Shalmaneser, king of Assyria, discovered that Hoshea had two-timed them with So of Egypt, that was the last straw. Israel would soon be no more.

Israel's problem was simple: they chose the wrong ally. When Judah faced the same crushing armies of Assyria, they chose the Lord as their ally. In one night, the angel of the Lord laid to waste Assyria's great military force.

One of the themes that runs straight through the historical books of the Old Testament is that the battle is the Lord's. As we have seen when Moses sat on a mountaintop with two friends holding up his arms to fight the Amalekites (see Ex. 17:11), or when young David felled a great giant (see 1 Sam. 17:37), the battle is won by the Lord and not by human strength or power. In this case, we hear the same message as the king of Judah stands on the city wall and says to a much larger force, "We trust the Lord." Sadly, Judah did not remain consistent in that conviction!

Section Commentary

The Fall of Israel (2 Kings 17)

In 721 B.C. the last king of Israel faced the full wrath of the Assyrian Empire and the armies of Sargon II. For years Israel had paid tribute

Sargon II and a dignitary.

Marie-Lan Nguyen/Wikimedia Commons

to Assyria, but in a foolish play for independence, King Hoshea forged a secret alliance with Egypt. In response, the Assyrians attacked.

Standard Assyrian policy was to deport vanquished enemies. This spread the conquered foe throughout the empire and destroyed their sense of national identity. Carvings on the walls of Assyrian ruins depict what would happen to those who fell in defeat. Assyria had refined the art of torture and humiliation. Friezes display soldiers piling severed heads, impaling bodies on spears, skinning people alive, and for the lucky ones, forcing steel hooks through the nose and leading them into exile like oxen, often with severed hands, feet, tongues, or ears.

Israel was too hard-hearted to realize that the real reason for their downfall had nothing to do with politics gone wrong. They were not victims of poor statesmanship. No, they had tolerated an unbroken string of nineteen idolatrous kings. For the wealthy and powerful among the Israelite elite, a healthy economy had kept them content in their spiritual adultery — until the Assyrian army arrived, knocking on their door, and it was too late to change.

Taking a Stand (2 Kings 18 – 19)

In sharp contrast to Israel, Judah chose the Lord as their ally. When Sargon II's successor, Sennacherib, camped outside the walls of Jerusalem, Judah might have sensed their doom was near. In pride the Assyrian ruler proclaimed that no god could save God's people.

But Hezekiah knew that God alone would determine the outcome of that conflict. He went into the temple and "spread [Sennacherib's threatening letter] out before the LORD" (19:14). In many ways, his actions here were reminiscent of Moses'. How many times had that leader, when the people gathered together in mutiny, fallen on his face and asked the Lord to intervene? The Lord heard Hezekiah's prayer. Without lifting a sword, Judah saw a hundred and eighty-five thousand soldiers of Assyria die at the hand of the Lord's avenging angel. Shortly after this Sennacherib, the greatest of the Assyrian kings, was assassinated in the temple of his god.

A Prophet Called Out (Isaiah 6)

Isaiah's vision of the heavenly throne is rich with gospel truth. The gospel first confronts us with our sin in light of God's holiness. Isaiah

Part of the Balawat gate from the palace of Shalmaneser III shows the cruel practices of war, including impaling bodies of the enemy.

sees the Lord and cries, "Woe is me!" He calls himself a man of "unclean lips." Then an angel takes a coal from the altar. This is significant because the altar was the place of sacrifice. Centuries later, the cross would become the final altar of sacrifice, where the blood of the Lamb of God was shed for sinners (see John 1:29). Like Isaiah, the best response to being saved from our sin is to respond to God's call to be sent. Isaiah cries out, "Here am I. Send me!" And that's what the Lord did, sending Isaiah out to speak truth to his nation.

The Very Bad News (Isaiah 13)

Even as they witnessed the Lord's mighty power, the people of Judah continued in rebellious idolatry. Although kings like Hezekiah attempted to cleanse the nation of idols, removing shrines and knocking down idols, the hearts of the people did not turn fully to the Lord. Isaiah proclaims the bad news to the people: the Lord himself will gather an army to destroy Jerusalem.

The Very Good News
(Isaiah 14, 49, 53)

Like no other prophet, Isaiah spoke of a future when not only Israel, but people from many nations would join together to worship the Lord in Jerusalem. These people would be set free from oppression. The God who brought punishment and sent them into exile would one day bring them back home! And he would do even more than free them from exile. He would provide a Servant to free them from the weight of sin. Isaiah gave the clearest Old Testament description of the Messiah. Isaiah prophesied —

- the coming of the Messiah (40:3 – 5)
- the virgin birth (7:14)
- that the Messiah would minister in Galilee (9:1 – 2)
- of the Messiah's deity and eternal throne (9:6 – 7)
- of the Messiah's sufferings (53)
- that the Messiah would die with sinners (53:9)
- that the Messiah would be buried in a rich man's tomb (53:9)
- that the Messiah's rule would be both mighty and gentle (40:10 – 11)
- that the Messiah would be a righteous king (32:1 – 8; 61:1 – 3)
- that the Messiah would be just and kind (42:3 – 4, 7)
- that the Messiah would rule over not only Israel but over the Gentiles as well (2:2 – 3; 42:1, 6; 49:6; 55:4 – 5; 60:3 – 5)
- that the Messiah would have great influence (49:7, 23)
- that idols would disappear (2:18)
- that under the Messiah's rule, there would be no more war (2:4; 65:25)
- that death would be destroyed (25:8; 26:19)
- that God's people would receive a new name (62:2; 65:15)
- that there would be a new heaven and new earth (65:17; 66:22)
- that the righteous and wicked would be eternally separated (66:15, 22 – 24)

It is no surprise that he is the most quoted source in the New Testament.

Discussion Questions

1. How does Isaiah describe the Lord's death in Isaiah 53? According to the passage, who is punishing Jesus and why?

2. How does the decisive and complete judgment of Israel square with the goodness of God? How does it challenge modern attitudes about God?

17

THE KINGDOMS' FALL

Plot Points

- God will not tolerate a wicked nation indefinitely.
- God's people, who had been brought into the Promised Land because the former occupants were so wicked, were now even more evil than the Canaanites had been.
- Even though it seems as if hope is dead, the Lord can breathe new life into dry bones.

Cast of Characters

Amon. Son of Manasseh; fourteenth king of Judah; an unrepentant sinner; assassinated; name means "workman"; did evil before the Lord.

Ezekiel. A priest; son of a priest named Buzi; deported to Babylon in 597 B.C.; gifted writer and prophet; prophesied to the exiles; name means "God strengthens."

Gedaliah. Governor appointed by Nebuchadnezzar after most of the people had been deported; name means "God is my greatness."

Jehoahaz. Third son of Josiah; sixteenth king of Judah; ruled only three months; an idolater; deposed by Pharaoh Necho and made prisoner in Egypt, where

The Kingdom of Judah (930–586 B.C.)

Kings	Prophets
930–913 Rehoboam	875–850 Elijah
872–848 Jehoshaphat	850–800 Elisha
715–686 Hezekiah	740–681 Isaiah
697–642 Manasseh	626–585 Jeremiah
640–609 Josiah	605–530 Daniel
609–598 Jehoiakim	593–571 Ezekiel
597–586 Zedekiah	
586 Fall of Jerusalem	

he died; name means "God has grasped";
did evil before the Lord.

Jehoiachin. Son of Jehoiakim; eighteenth king
of Judah; taken prisoner by Nebuchadnezzar; name means "God will establish"; did
evil before the Lord.

Jehoiakim. Son of Jehoahaz; seventeenth king
of Judah; made a vassal of Nebuchadnez-

zar; left Judah significantly weaker; a cruel
and greedy king; name means "God estab-
lishes"; did evil before the Lord.

Jeremiah. Major prophet during the reigns of
the last five kings of Judah; began ministry
under Josiah; imprisoned by kings and rescued from dungeons; prophesied and saw
the downfall of Jerusalem; exiled to Egypt;

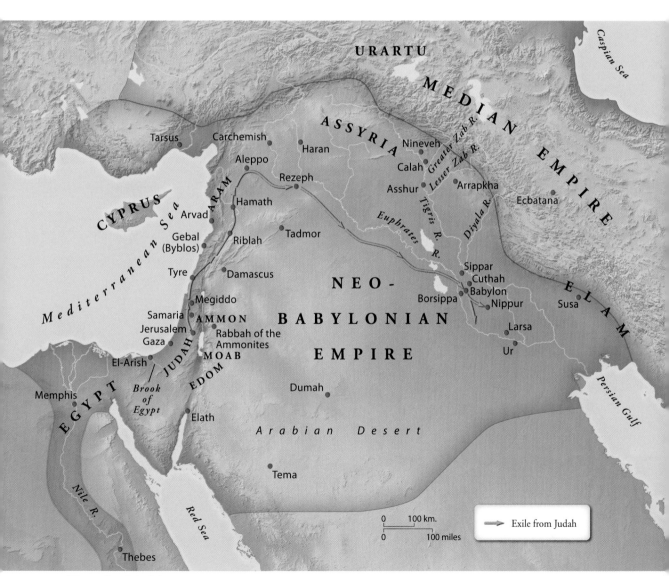

The exile of Judah.

called the "weeping prophet"; name means "God is high."

Josiah. Son of Amon; sixteenth king of Judah; discovered the Book of the Law of Moses and led Israel in reform; died in battle against Pharaoh Necho in 609 b.c.; did right before the Lord.

Manasseh. Son of King Hezekiah; fourteenth king of Judah; did not walk in the ways of his father; led all of Israel into idolatry, rebuilding the altars to Baal and Asherah that his father had destroyed; "filled Jerusalem from end to end" with innocent blood (2 Kings 21:16); repented and was forgiven; did evil before the Lord.

Nebuchadnezzar. King of Babylon; most powerful king of the empire; destroyed Jerusalem and led captives into exile; suffered madness for four or seven years as punishment for his pride; name means "Nebo is the protector against misfortune."

Nebuzaradan. Commander of Nebuchadnezzar's imperial guard.

Pashhur. Son of Malkijah; sent by Zedekiah to inquire of Jeremiah the prophet.

Zedekiah. Nineteenth and final king of Judah; a wicked king who ignored Jeremiah's prophecy; installed by Nebuchadnezzar after Jehoiachin was removed; rebelled against Nebuchadnezzar, leading to the siege of Jerusalem; blinded and led into exile; name means "Jehovah is mighty"; did evil before the Lord.

Zephaniah. Son of Maaseiah; sent by Zedekiah to inquire of Jeremiah the prophet.

Chapter Overview

In the beginning God created a perfect home for humans, a garden named Eden. He asked them to trust and obey him by not eating the fruit of a certain tree. When they disobeyed and ate the fruit they were expelled from their garden home. Sin spread throughout the world and infected the descendants of Adam and Eve so thoroughly that the only answer was annihilation, yet God saved one family. Setting them down in a world scraped clean, he asked them to spread out and once again fill the earth. Yet again they disobeyed, and the Lord struck confusion in their midst, confounding their communication and multiplying

Musee des Beaux-Arts, Rennes, France/Giraudon/The Bridgeman Art Library International

King Manasseh pictured with Amon and Josiah.

their languages. By the time of Abraham, no one was serving the Creator God any longer.

But in calling Abraham, the Lord made a covenant with a chosen people. He made promises to Abraham and his children forever. In 1 Kings 4:20 we read that the people of Abraham grew "as numerous as the sand on the seashore." God's promises to Abraham were fulfilled as his descendants grew and inherited the Promised Land.

Unfortunately, after receiving the promises of God, the pattern of sin repeated once again. Just as it happened in the garden, and after the days of the flood, it was happening again. God had made a good place for his people, but his people did not trust his guidelines or accept his direction. Once again, God would have to clean out his house and start again.

Section Commentary

Even Worse Than Before
(2 Kings 21, 23, 24; 2 Chronicles 33)

An ancient tradition claims that Manasseh put Isaiah to death. According to the story, this wicked king stretched out the ninety-two-year-old prophet between two pieces of wood and sawed him in half. The early church fathers believed this event is referenced in Hebrews 11. Whether or not this actually happened, Scripture does record that Manasseh offered his own son as a human sacrifice and built pagan altars in the temple. In other words, Manasseh was a bad man.

But he was really just the tip of the iceberg. Manasseh was surrounded by a political system that actively tried to drive the true worship of God out of Israel. Of the six kings who ruled after Manasseh before the fall of Judah, only one of them even tried to turn Judah around. The situation grew so desperate that the Lord declared that Judah had become as wicked as the people who were in the Promised Land before Israel — the Canaanites. In other words, the people God had used to cleanse the land of evil were now in need of cleansing themselves!

Against the Mountains
(Ezekiel 1–2, 6–7)

The opening chapter of Ezekiel is filled with strange imagery. We read of big wheels, bizarre creatures, and a strange throne. It is helpful to compare the description of images in this passage with Revelation 1:12–17 and 4:1–11. Each passage gives a slightly different perspective on the same thing: God's throne. In Ezekiel, though the images are strange and somewhat confusing, the message is simple: Ezekiel, you are being called into a difficult ministry, but trust that the Lord is on the throne! Be brave! It certainly would take courage to confront the wickedness of the nation. After all, Jerusalem was no longer a city that welcomed those who spoke for God. It had become a city that killed prophets.

The message Ezekiel spoke would not be popular either. He was called to communicate a message of coming destruction. The altars and high places people took for granted were in God's crosshairs, and his people were on their way to exile.

Courage to Confront
(Jeremiah 1–2, 4–5, 13)

As with Ezekiel, God called Jeremiah to be courageous in his calling. And he was, even as a young man. One of the central images of Jeremiah's prophecy is the choice between fresh

An artist's interpretation of the destruction of Jerusalem.

springwater and stale cistern water. In choosing to live in idolatry, God's people have opted for the latter.

No Remedy (2 Kings 25; 2 Chronicles 36; Jeremiah 21)

Eventually, the cup of God's wrath was filled to the tipping point, and his judgment upon Jerusalem began. Nebuchadnezzar brought the armies of Babylon to Jerusalem and put the city under a two-year siege. Ezekiel describes what that was like in 5:8 – 12 (NIV):

"Therefore this is what the Sovereign LORD says: I myself am against you, Jerusalem, and I will inflict punishment on you in the sight of the nations. Because of all your detestable idols, I will do to you what I have never done before and will never do again. Therefore in your midst parents will eat their children, and children will eat their parents. I will inflict punishment on you and will scatter all your survivors to the winds. Therefore as surely as I live, declares the Sovereign LORD, because you have defiled my sanctuary with all your vile images and detestable practices, I myself will shave you; I will not look on you with pity or spare you. A third of your people will die of the plague or perish by famine inside you; a third will fall by the sword outside your walls; and a third I will scatter to the winds and pursue with drawn sword."

It was a terrible time to live, a time of suffering and destruction. For the generation that lived through the breaking of Jerusalem, there would be no remedy for their pain.

Lament (Lamentations 1 – 3, 5)

Can you remember what it was like when you first heard news of a great disaster like 9/11 or saw the horrific destruction caused by Hurricane Katrina? Many people were glued to their TV sets when the Twin Towers fell and when the stormy winds brought floods and devastation to the Gulf Coast. Some experienced the destruction firsthand and lived through those days, an experience they will not forget and certainly would not want to repeat.

Although Jeremiah knew the day of judgment would eventually come, nothing could prepare him for the experience itself. He wept for the city. He wept for the temple. But more than anything, he wept at the waste. If only God's people had turned from their sin!

For My Holy Name (Ezekiel 36 – 37)

Both Jeremiah and Ezekiel had unflinchingly prophesied the destruction of Jerusalem. They had spoken graphically about the horrors the people would suffer, and they both knew that it was God's perfect justice at work. At the same time, after Jerusalem had fallen and the days of judgment were over, their message became one of hope and restoration: "This land that was laid waste has become like the garden of Eden" (Ezek. 36:35). Despite God's anger and his judgment against the sin of his people, there was still hope for the future. God had not abandoned his promises to Abraham and David!

Discussion Questions

1. How does the story of the Promised Land echo the story of the garden of Eden?

2. How much responsibility did the leadership in Judah bear for the people's apostasy? Explain.

3. How do the themes addressed in the prophetic passages confront the church in America?

18

DANIEL IN EXILE

Plot Points

- God is sovereign over the events of our lives and world empires.
- Daniel and his friends were called to a difficult task: to be a holy people in an unholy culture.
- As seen in the lives of Nebuchadnezzar and Belshazzar, pride is always punished.
- God *never* abandons his people, whether they are in a lion's den, a fiery furnace, or exile.

Cast of Characters

Arioch. Commander of the king's guard under Nebuchadnezzar.

Ashpenaz. Chief of court officials under Nebuchadnezzar.

Azariah. Carried away into exile under Nebuchadnezzar; given the name Abednego ("servant of Nego") by his Babylonian captors; an attendant and adviser to King Nebuchadnezzar; lived through a fiery ordeal; a friend of Daniel; name means "he who hears the Lord."

Belshazzar. Last king of Babylon; saw strange writing on his wall during a profane feast; name means "Bel protect the king."

The Kingdom of Judah

Judah (930–586 B.C.)	The Neo-Babylonian Period (625–539 B.C.)
605–530 Daniel	626–605 Nabopolassar 605–562 Nebuchadnezzar 555–539 Nabonidus (Note: Belshazzar was the son of Nabonidus and ruled in Babylon on his father's behalf) 539 Babylon falls to Persia 539–530 Cyrus

Cyrus. Founded the Persian Empire and allowed the Jews to return to Jerusalem and begin rebuilding.

Daniel. Carried away into exile under Nebuchadnezzar; given the name Belteshazzar ("prince of Bel") by his Babylonian captors; cast into the lions' den for praying to God; prophesied about the rise and fall of great empires; name means "who is like God" or "God is my judge."

Darius the Mede. Perhaps the Babylonian throne name of Cyrus; appointed Daniel to a high position in his government.

Hananiah. Carried away into exile under Nebuchadnezzar; given the name Shadrach ("tender") by his Babylonian captors; an attendant and adviser to King Nebuchadnezzar; lived through a fiery ordeal; a friend of Daniel; name means "grace, mercy, gift of the Lord."

Jeremiah. Major prophet during the reigns of the last five kings of Judah; began ministry under Josiah; imprisoned by kings and rescued from dungeons; prophesied and saw the downfall of Jerusalem; exiled to Egypt; called the "weeping prophet"; name means "God is high."

Mishael. Carried away into exile under Nebuchadnezzar; given the name Meshach ("that draws with force") by his Babylonian captors; an attendant and adviser to King Nebuchadnezzar; lived through a fiery ordeal; a friend of Daniel; name means "who is asked for."

Nebuchadnezzar. King of Babylon; most powerful king of the empire; destroyed Jerusalem and led captives into exile; suffered madness for four or seven years as punishment for his pride; name means "Nebo is the protector against misfortune."

Chapter Overview

Daniel and his fellow exiles faced a daunting challenge. How could they live as holy people in the midst of an unholy culture? The vision and values of Babylon were not those of the covenant community. They constantly interacted and worked with people who embraced false gods, lived sinful lives, and approached everyday existence with a radically different set of norms. Daniel, Hananiah, Mishael, and Azariah provide a powerful example of how God's people can live faithfully in the midst of a sinful, ungodly culture.

They resisted bitterness. Consider how difficult this would have been for them. They had been dragged away to a foreign land, possibly made eunuchs, and thrown into service for a king they despised and hated. Yet rather than growing bitter, they made themselves useful.

They always remained respectful. Rather than simply "taking a stand," they approached their peers and superiors with humility. At the same time, they absolutely refused to compromise on the nonnegotiables. If it meant fire or lions, they were willing to sacrifice.

Ultimately, they maintained hope in God's Word. Daniel was aware of Jeremiah's prophecy: in seventy years the exile would end. Daniel's hope was not in his ability to change his circumstances. His hope was in the sovereign Lord and his promise. Armed with that hope, Daniel and his friends were able to live lives of significance, even in an unholy culture.

Section Commentary

Belly of the Beast (Daniel 1)

Daniel was probably fifteen or sixteen when he was taken to Babylon. He would spend the rest

A Russian icon depicting Nebuchadnezzar while Shadrach, Meshak, and Abednego are in the fiery furnace.

fifty-three temples in the fantastic "city of gold."

Daniel and his friends had entered a new world. As young, teenage men, no one was looking over their shoulders any longer. The easiest way to make it in this new home would have been simply to go with the flow. But that is not what they did. They humbly refused to cave on their convictions, choosing to follow God's ways rather than adopting the practices of the Babylonians. And it all started with something quite ordinary and normal: the very food they ate.

Dreams (Daniel 2)

As we have seen already in the story, dreams were a valued source of revelation in the ancient Near East. Nebuchadnezzar's dream in Daniel 2 ranks among the most significant in recorded history! Nebuchadnezzar was given a sweeping glimpse of four great empires spanning more than five hundred years, culminating in the establishment of God's kingdom on earth. These empires are generally understood to be the Babylonian, Persian, Greek, and Roman Empires. Some believe that the partly iron, partly clay toes seen in the dream indicate a time in the future, or they are identified with yet another historical empire.

It is worth noting how Daniel conducted himself in this scene. Take special note of his humble approach. When Arioch, the com-

of his life far from home, disconnected from his family, living in what at the time was the most powerful city in the world. With walls three hundred feet high, eighty feet thick, and sinking thirty-five feet below ground to prevent undermining, Babylon was a wonder of the ancient world. It was the capital of pagan worship, where the great temple of Marduk connected with the tower of Babylon (perhaps the ancient Tower of Babel). Contained within the temple was a golden image of Marduk and a table weighing at least fifty thousand pounds. That was just one of

mander of the king's guard, was preparing to carry out the orders of execution, Daniel spoke to him "with wisdom and tact" (v. 14). Throughout his life, Daniel proved humble and useful to these pagan kings. This opened the door for him to speak boldly at critical times, as he did while standing before Nebuchadnezzar: "There is a God in heaven who reveals mysteries" (v. 28). In context, this was a bold statement. Daniel was essentially telling King Nebuchadnezzar, "Marduk did not give you this dream, and his priestly minions cannot explain it. But YHWH did and can." Daniel reminds us that speaking the truth does not mean that we need to be caustic and annoying. A humble spirit can open doors to boldly present God's message!

Decisions (Daniel 3)

Perhaps twenty years separate the story of the king's dream and the events we read about in this section. Daniel and his friends had become established figures in the kingdom. Sadly, it appears Nebuchadnezzar had forgotten his earlier, humbler response to the Lord, "Surely your God is the God of gods and the Lord of kings and a revealer of mysteries, for you were able to reveal this mystery" (Dan. 2:47).

The Lord chose to use three brave men to again remind the king who was really in charge. He did it in a very public way. At the dedication ceremony for Nebuchadnezzar's obscene image, before all the gathered dignitaries, Hananiah, Mishael, and Azariah refused

Giorces/Wikimedia Commons

This fourth-century A.D. mosaic shows Daniel in the lions' den.

to bow. The king's decision to throw them in the furnace was meant to be a clear statement to everyone watching: "This is what happens to those who cross my will and dishonor my decrees." The Lord God, however, miraculously saved the three young men from death in the fire of the furnace. That day God made his own statement to King Nebuchadnezzar: "This is what happens to those who give their ultimate loyalty to me!"

The Cyrus Cylinder records the fall of Babylon.

A Message for the New King
(Daniel 6)

During the more than seventy years that Daniel served the king in Babylon, he had been a witness to the truth about God. God had used Daniel and his friends to mediate his word to these pagan kings, interpreting dreams and words scratched on walls. Now, under the rule of Darius, God used this ninety-year-old man to communicate to the ruler of the world's great empire. The lion was a symbol of imperial strength and power, hunted in the parks of the kings. When a ruler hunted the lion, he showed his supremacy. Through Daniel, the Lord showed the Persian ruler that God alone is the King of Kings.

Unshakable Promise (Jeremiah 29–31)

God's promises, not our current circumstances, should set the horizon line of our hope. It is tempting to evaluate what is possible in light of the immediate. We look around at our present circumstances and assume they have the power to control tomorrow. But Jeremiah's prophecy reminded Israel, as it reminds us, that the Lord is sovereign over human history. If he has promised something, then he will do it.

Discussion Questions

1. How do you think the story of Daniel and his friends would have served to encourage the Israelites in exile?

2. As you read Daniel's story, what are the chief character qualities that emerge? How were these important in his calling?

THE RETURN HOME

19

Plot Points

- The sovereign Lord can move the heart of an emperor to accomplish his purposes.
- The Lord's steadfast love and covenant faithfulness should *never* be doubted, and his prophecies always come to pass.
- God's people will always face opposition in achieving a worthwhile task, but they can rely on the Lord to see them through as they faithfully labor.

Cast of Characters

Artaxerxes. King of Persia; had Ezra and Nehemiah in his court; name means "the silence of the light."

Cyrus. Founded the Persian Empire and allowed the Jews to return to Jerusalem and begin rebuilding the temple.

Darius III. King of Persia during the time of Nehemiah.

Haggai. A minor prophet; one of three prophets who ministered after the return from captivity; contrasted the opulence of the people's homes with the ruined state of the temple; name means "born on a feast day."

Joshua. Son of Jozadak; high priest and contemporary of Zerubbabel.

The Return (538–432 B.C.)

Biblical	Secular
538 First group returns under Zerubbabel	559–530 Cyrus
520–480 Zechariah	530–522 Cambyses
516 Temple completed	522–486 Darius I
478 Esther becomes queen	486–465 Xerxes I (Ahasuerus)
458 Second group returns under Ezra	464–423 Artaxerxes I
444 Nehemiah rebuilds the wall	
440–430 Malachi	
432 Last group returns under Nehemiah	

Nebuchadnezzar. King of Babylon; most powerful king of the empire; destroyed Jerusalem and led captives into exile; suffered madness for four or seven years as punishment for his pride; name means "Nebo is the protector against misfortune."

Sheshbazzar. Son of Shealtiel; grandson of Jehoiachin, Judah's next-to-last king; also called Zerubbabel ("seed of Babylon"); governor of Judah during the return; directed during the rebuilding of the temple; name means "joy in tribulation."

Shethar-Bozenai. Associate of Tattenai who worked with him to halt the rebuilding of the temple.

Tattenai. Governor of the Trans-Euphrates region; attempted to stop Israel from rebuilding the temple.

Zechariah. Prophet who encouraged Israel to continue work on the temple; son of Berekiah; grandson of Iddo.

This royal inscription of Xerxes is written in Old Persian. It reads, "I [am] Xerxes the great King, the King of kings, the King of countries having many [kinds of] human beings, the King in this great earth far and wide, the son of Darius the King, an Achaemenian."

Chapter Overview

The Lord himself had used Babylon to destroy his temple. He had wielded the armies of that empire like a weapon of war (see Jer. 21:4–5). But now God was leading his people home. He was bringing them back to rebuild the temple.

Notice how little God's people actually had to do to make the rebuilding of the temple happen. God influenced pagan kings to provide all the supplies that were needed. In addition, these foreign rulers not only provided materials but protection as well.

The Lord asked his people for only one thing: to remain faithful in the work. Israel was called to pray, worship, and labor faithfully — and God would take care of the rest. But like so many times before, this proved too difficult for them.

They faced opposition from without and apathy from within and failed to obey God's directions yet again. As he had in the past, the Lord sent prophets once again to spur the people forward.

The moving story of the exiles' return is punctuated most poignantly when the foundation of the temple is laid. While the younger generation cheered, the older ones wept, recognizing just how meager the new footprint of the temple really was. Compared to the former glory and magnificence of Solomon's temple, it was a mere shadow of the past. This reminds us of another theme in God's story: until the Lord himself returns, everything we build will be marked by the brokenness of this fallen world! But when he returns, the true temple will be revealed and God's work seen in its true beauty.

Section Commentary

Coming Home Again (Ezra 1)

It is helpful to understand how the stages of the return unfolded:

First, for twenty years under Zerubbabel as governor and Joshua as priest, the temple was rebuilt. This period is covered in Ezra 3 – 6.

Haggai and Zechariah prophesied at that time. Second, for twenty-five years, under Nehemiah as governor and Ezra as priest, the walls were rebuilt. This period unfolded in two stages: first, when Ezra returned for initial work on the walls; and second, a short time later, when Nehemiah assumed leadership as governor and brought the full support of the Persian bank to

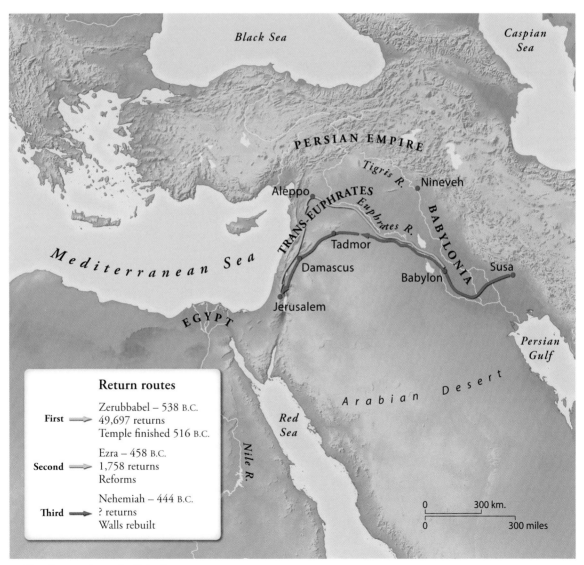

Black Sea

Caspian Sea

PERSIAN EMPIRE

Tigris R.

Nineveh

Aleppo

TRANS-EUPHRATES

Euphrates R.

BABYLONIA

Tadmor

Damascus

Babylon

Susa

Mediterranean Sea

Jerusalem

EGYPT

Persian Gulf

Arabian Desert

Red Sea

Nile R.

Return routes

First → Zerubbabel – 538 B.C.
49,697 returns
Temple finished 516 B.C.

Second → Ezra – 458 B.C.
1,758 returns
Reforms

Third → Nehemiah – 444 B.C.
? returns
Walls rebuilt

0   300 km.

0   300 miles

The three returns to Palestine.

A bull's head from the time of Xerxes and Artaxerxes I.

Todd Bolen/www.BiblePlaces.com

the project. While Malachi prophesied during this time, Ezra provided a history of both periods and Nehemiah of the second. The story of Esther falls some time between these two latter periods.

Building the Temple (Ezra 3–4)

As they had at the dedication of Solomon's temple, the people of Israel gathered to celebrate when the foundation of the new temple was laid. Their simple, profound proclamation of the Lord's goodness and steadfast love echoed that of their ancestors four hundred years before. This moment of joy is also marked by the painful realization that the restored temple is not what it once was.

Priorities (Haggai 1–2; Zechariah 1, 8)

At Mount Sinai Israel had stood and proclaimed their intention to be God's covenant people. They committed themselves to obeying his commands. But the forty days Moses spent on the mountaintop gave them too much free time! So they partied and prostrated themselves before an idol instead.

While the situation is not quite as dire in the time of Haggai and Zechariah, the people are following a similar pattern. They are quickly abandoning their commitment to obey the Lord and are choosing to satisfy their own needs instead. Rather than finishing a difficult work, they have settled in on padding their own nests. God uses the prophets Haggai and Zechariah to remind the people of their commitment to God and spur them on again.

Whatever Is Needed (Ezra 5 – 6)

Any worthy task will encounter opposition. The first time Israel faced difficulties in rebuilding the temple, they grew discouraged and laid down their tools. But thanks to the prophetic words of Haggai and Zechariah, the people soon resumed their work. This time, when they encountered opposition, the people remained steadfast, and the Lord once again demonstrated his power and sovereignty.

Rather than stopping the rebuilding, the opponents served as a catalyst for completion! In fact, their efforts to roadblock the process of rebuilding had the opposite effect: establishing Israel's right to rebuild and reinforcing the empire's commitment to finance and protect the project. After fifteen years of setbacks, the temple was completed in just four years! On March 12, 516 B.C., seventy years after the temple's destruction, a new temple was dedicated in Jerusalem. The Lord kept his covenant promise and demonstrated his steadfast love for his people.

Discussion Questions

1. What roadblocks did God's people encounter in rebuilding the temple? How were they able to keep moving forward in spite of the opposition?

2. What indications of the Lord's favor were they given?

3. Do you find it easy or difficult to keep moving toward a worthy goal in spite of opposition? Why?

20

THE QUEEN OF BEAUTY AND COURAGE

Plot Points

- While Esther and Mordecai are God's key players, it is God himself who stands out as the sovereign hero in this story.
- In Esther's example, we see that God calls his people fearlessly to risk all for what is right.
- In Haman's demise, we see a perfect illustration of an eternal truth: pride goes before a fall.

Cast of Characters

Bigthana and Teresh. Two officers in Xerxes' guard; caught by Mordecai in an assassination plot against the king.

Habrona. One of Xerxes' eunuchs; suggested Haman be impaled on the stake he had erected for Mordecai.

Hadassah. Daughter of Abihail; also known as Esther ("secret; hidden"); adopted by her cousin Mordecai; became queen to Xerxes when Vashti had been deposed; saved her people from annihilation at the hands of Haman, a homicidal noble in Xerxes' court; name means "a myrtle, joy."

Haman. Son of Hammedatha, a descendant of Agag, the Amalekite King Saul did not kill; an influential noble in Xerxes' court; plotted to kill all Jews because of his grudge against Mordecai; executed when his plot was exposed by Esther.

The Return (538–432 B.C.)

Biblical	Secular
516 Temple completed	486–465 Xerxes I (Ahasuerus)
478 Esther becomes queen	464–423 Artaxerxes I
458 Second group returns under Ezra	

Haman's sons. Parshandatha, Dalphon, Aspatha, Poratha, Adalia, Aridatha, Parmashta, Arisai, Aridai, Vaizatha; killed by the Jews whom Xerxes had authorized to act in self-defense.

Hathak. One of Xerxes' eunuchs; assigned to attend Esther.

Hegai. The king's eunuch, responsible for Xerxes' harem.

Karshena, Shethar, Admatha, Tarshish, Meres, Marsena. Persian nobles, responsible for advising Xerxes.

Mehuman, Biztha, Harbona, Bigtha, Abagtha, Zethar, Karkas. Eunuchs and servants of Xerxes.

Memukan. Persian noble, advised Xerxes to divorce Queen Vashti and find a new queen.

Mordecai. Son of Jair; grandson of Shimei; great-grandson of Kish, who had been brought into exile by Nebuchadnezzar; cousin and adoptive father to Esther; name means "contrition."

Queen Vashti. Wife of Xerxes; lost her position when she refused to appear before the king and his guests.

Shaashgaz. Xerxes' eunuch in charge of the concubines.

Xerxes. Emperor of the Persian Empire; also called Ahasuerus; married Esther; ruled over 127 provinces from India to Cush.

Zeresh. Wife of Haman; name means "misery, dispersed inheritance."

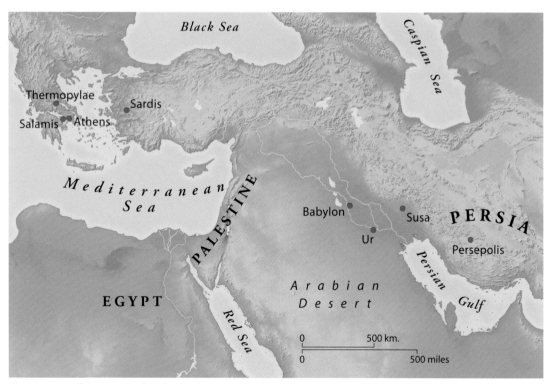

The setting of the story of Esther.

Chapter Overview

Curiously, the story of Esther never explicitly references God. How strange for a book in the Bible! And yet, though God is never referenced we see evidence of his presence, power, and protection everywhere in this fast-paced novella.

The theme of God's *sovereignty* shines through in the arrangement of events. Because Queen Vashti was deposed, Esther was raised up. And because Esther was raised up, she was in a position to save her people. The Lord was clearly arranging events for a purpose.

We also see that God *uses people* to accomplish his purpose. Although he can directly alter history, as he had done in past events in Israel's history, God also changes the course of history through the choices and actions of people. Mordecai, Esther's older cousin, cared for her, raised her and advised her. When the time was critical, he exhorted her to be courageous. Esther could see what needed to happen to save her people, but she had to be brave to make it happen!

God's justice is clearly on display as well. Haman is the archetypal villain: proud, diabolical, and ruthless. In the end, he is impaled on his own stake. Justice is served.

Most importantly, we see that God is preserving his people. While he brings punishment and suffering in response to Israel's disobedience, the Lord does not allow *any* power to annihilate them. There are still promises waiting to be fulfilled. In particular, the Lord has promised Abraham that one of his descendants will bring blessing to all nations.

Section Commentary

Finding a Queen (Esther 1 – 2)

The palace at Susa, two hundred miles east of Babylon, was the winter residence of the Persian kings. The opulence of the empire is attested in many sources. Herodotus reported that Darius received fourteen thousand talents of gold in tribute each year (one Greek talent = fifty-seven pounds). When Alexander the Great plundered Persia and Babylon, he measured one hundred eighty thousand talents of gold and silver. The drunken revelry described in this story was common in pagan courts. In fact, Herodotus also claimed the Persians would seek intoxication when making political decisions because they believed it connected them to the spiritual world.

In this context it is no surprise that an extravagant process would be proposed for finding a new queen. It has been suggested that Xerxes deposed Vashti, went on a military campaign, and returned home while the search for the new queen took place. Thirteen years after his marriage to Esther, Xerxes died. Esther was certainly swept up into another world when she was chosen as a candidate and then selected as the queen of the empire!

© Xuan Che

A golden rhyton from the Oxus treasure in Achaemenid, Persia.

A relief from Persepolis, depicting Xerxes, 470 B.C. There is still debate as to whether the king seated is Darius, with Xerxes standing behind, or if Xerxes is seated, with the crown prince standing behind.

Two King's Men (Esther 2–4)

The contrast between Haman and Mordecai could not be clearer. Throughout the story, we see that Haman is a man of pride. As a key player in Persian politics, he uses his position to elevate himself above others. He wields his power to settle petty disputes with overwhelming force. In short, Haman is all about Haman.

On the other hand, Mordecai, himself a royal official, is a man of humility. He uses his position to *protect* the king from assassination. He risks his life to preserve his people. For those familiar with God's story, it comes as no surprise that Haman ends up on a stake and Mordecai in an elevated position.

A Risky Move (Esther 5)

Other sources confirm that Persian kings limited access to the throne room. Herodotus wrote that only seven noble families were allowed entry. Other sources record that access would be granted only with the permission of the *hazarpatish*, the head of the king's bodyguard. It is possible that Haman held this position, making it impossible for Esther to request permission to enter the king's presence.

Skewered (Esther 6–7)

The author of Esther has a finely tuned sense of irony! He highlights how Haman was placed in increasingly frustrating situations, always coming out the loser to Mordecai. First, Mordecai refused to bow to him without consequence. Next, believing he was to be honored by the king, Haman dreamed up a wish list of honors for himself, but he ended up honoring his rival Mordecai instead. Finally, in the final twist to the story, Haman was himself impaled on the seventy-five-foot-high stake he had erected for Mordecai. Although he never realized it, Haman was not simply fighting Mordecai. His true adversary was the Lord he dishonored by his prideful heart and selfish drive to murder and destroy the Lord's servants.

Tables Turned (Esther 8 – 10)

As we saw in Daniel (8:8), the decree of a Persian king could not be overturned. Although Haman had been dispatched, the decree to massacre the Jews still stood. This story hauntingly resonates with the events of twentieth-century Germany under the Nazi regime. In Esther's time, however, the Jews were able to rise up and defend themselves. To this day Jewish people memorialize this great event in the Feast of Purim.

Discussion Questions

1. Where did Mordecai and Esther turn when faced with a difficult situation? What do we learn from their actions?

2. What specific convictions do you think Esther had to maintain as she risked her life in facing the king?

3. What specific convictions do you believe are required for living faithfully in our world today?

21

REBUILDING THE WALLS

Plot Points

- God's sovereign hand is at work, preserving his people and paving the way to blessing if they chose to obey.
- The Word of God brings revival and reformation to the covenant community.
- God's purposes are accomplished through the hard work of prayer, the sweat of faithful labor, and the courage to stand and fight.
- The people of God cannot dwell in his Promised Land as faithful witnesses if they are living compromised lives, failing in matters of basic obedience and ethical integrity.

Cast of Characters

Artaxerxes I. King of Persia; stepson of Esther; had Ezra and Nehemiah in his court; name means "the silence of the light."

Ezra. Prophet, priest and teacher of the Law; great-grandson of Hilkiah the priest, who had directed King Josiah's reformation; returned to Jerusalem to teach the law; name means "help."

Geshem. An associate of Sanballat and Tobiah; joined with Sanballat in a scheme to assassinate Nehemiah.

Levite teachers. Jeshua, Bani, Sherebiah, Jamin, Akkub, Shabbethai, Hodiah, Maaseiah, Kelita, Azariah, Jozabad, Hanan, Pelaiah; taught people from the Book of the Law.

The Return (538–432 B.C.)

Biblical	Secular
458 Second group returns under Ezra	486–465 Xerxes I (Esther his queen)
444 Nehemiah rebuilds the wall	464–423 Artaxerxes I
440–430 Malachi	
432 Last group returns under Nehemiah	

Malachi. Last of the Old Testament prophets; probably a contemporary of Ezra and Nehemiah; name means "my messenger."

Nehemiah. Son of Hakaliah; cupbearer to the king of Persia; governor of Jerusalem; organized rebuilding of city walls; name means "the Lord comforts."

Sanballat. Governor of Samaria; attempted to stop Israel from rebuilding the wall of Jerusalem; name means "the god Sin has given life."

Shemiah. Son of Delaiah; grandson of Mehetable; name means "hears or obeys the Lord."

Tobiah. Leading official, perhaps governor, of Transjordan; joined with Sanballat in trying to undermine Israel's work to rebuild the walls of Jerusalem; name means "the Lord is good."

Chapter Overview

Fifty years earlier God had used the political leadership of Zerubbabel and the prophetic voices of Haggai and Zechariah to encourage Israel in rebuilding the temple. Now the Lord sent new leadership to help the people finish Jerusalem's walls.

At the heart of this chapter are the twin themes of preaching and prayer. Ezra, an anointed priest and teacher, was commissioned by the Lord to call the people to biblically faithful lives. He stood up, read the Law, and saw revival spread among the people. Nehemiah, who provided political leadership to the nation, was praying and seeking God's guidance at every turn, just like Moses before him.

In that same period, the prophet Malachi was

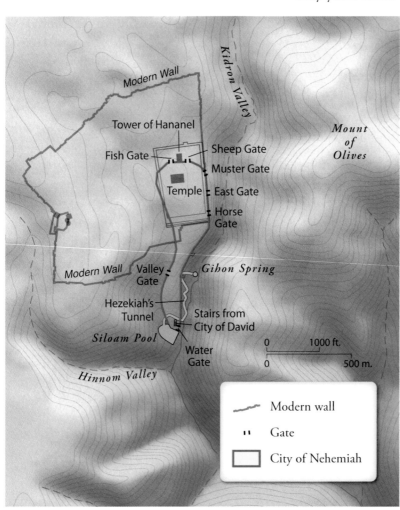

Jerusalem during the time of Nehemiah.

© Ilia Torlin/www.BigStockPhoto.com

Tombs of Persian kings near Persepolis. Artaxerxes I's tomb is shown on the far right.

raised up by God and serves as the last of the Old Testament prophets. He challenged the returned exiles not to be satisfied with half measures. After returning from exile to the Promised Land and rebuilding the temple, it would not do for God's people to compromise again!

Section Commentary

Sent on a Mission
(Ezra 7; Nehemiah 1–2)

For thirteen years Ezra had labored in Jerusalem. His calling was to teach God's Word to Israel. In the meantime, there was work left unfinished. The walls of the temple remained broken down and burned. To complement the spiritual leadership of Ezra, the Lord called Nehemiah, a royal official in Artaxerxes I's court, to provide political leadership to God's people. Nehemiah was a man of great administrative gifts, faithful prayer, vision, and action, and he proved a perfect complement to Ezra's role as preacher and spiritual teacher to the nation.

Although it is not mentioned in the Scriptures, we should not miss the connection between Esther and the events described in this chapter. It is almost certainly the case that Esther outlived her husband Xerxes and remained a prominent member of the royal court long into the reign of Artaxerxes I. As the king's stepmother, she would have continued to exert a powerful influence on the king directly responsible for helping rebuild Jerusalem. Perhaps his enthusiasm for the project can to some degree be attributed to her. The Lord's hand of providence over the future of his people continues ... even after the story has ended!

Opposition ... Again (Nehemiah 4, 6)

Once again, Israel experienced opposition to their rebuilding effort. Peoples who had been driven out centuries beforehand — Moabites, Ammonites, Ashdodites, and Samaritans — tried to halt progress and disrupt the work. Under Nehemiah's leadership, however, the people persisted and finished building the wall rather quickly — in a mere fifty-two days!

Reformation
(Nehemiah 7 – 8; Malachi 1 – 4)

God's Word is given to his people so that it can be proclaimed. The people could work and build their city, but unless their community was founded on the Word of God, they would inevitably fall into the same patterns that had led to their exile. We should note that the people themselves gathered together and asked Ezra to read from the Book of the Law, indicating a genuine thirst for truth and a heartfelt willingness to obey.

Malachi, whose ministry likely overlapped with Ezra and Nehemiah, confronted people who had been set adrift in the sea of spiritual compromise. He targeted several specific areas to challenge: First, the people were showing a great contempt for the sacrifices brought to the Lord. Instead of bringing the very best animals, they brought their worst. Second, the people were intermarrying with their pagan neighbors. Earlier, this had been a key reason for their drift into paganism. Finally, Malachi confronted their lack of faith in the area of finances. Despite God's promise to bless their cheerful giving, there was a skeptical unwillingness to bring in their tithes and offerings to support the Lord's work and show faithful obedience to his commands.

Malachi closed his prophecy with a promise: the day of the Lord is coming. Elijah will precede that day. And it will be a time of decision and division when people will have to choose between living for the Lord or losing everything.

Discussion Questions

1. How did Ezra and Nehemiah's respective roles complement each other? What does this tell us about spiritual gifts in the church?

2. How does Ezra serve as a model of biblically faithful preaching? What does this tell us about the importance of preaching in the church?

3. How might Malachi's prophetic insight apply to the church in America today?

THE BIRTH OF THE KING

22

Plot Points

- John explicitly teaches the preexistence of the Son of God, the Word who was with God and was God.
- Matthew emphasizes Jesus' birth to a virgin mother and adoptive father who, in faith, committed themselves to God's mysterious plan, including angelic visitors, important dreams, magi from far away, and a trip to Egypt.
- Luke demonstrates God's sovereign hand guiding history to fulfill prophecy and highlights the humble shepherds who visited Jesus.

Cast of Characters

Anna. A prophetess in Jerusalem; met baby Jesus when he was brought by Mary and Joseph for his presentation in the temple; name means "grace."

Archelaus. Son of Herod the Great; ruled over Idumea, Judea, and Samaria; name means "the prince of the people."

Caesar Augustus. Name of Emperor Octavian, nephew of Julius Caesar; ruled when Jesus was born; name means "august."

Gabriel. Angel sent to Mary to announce the birth of Jesus.

Herod. Herod the great; king of Judea when Jesus was born; a murderous ruler who posed as a Jewish king; built the temple Jesus worshiped in; name means "heroic."

Jesus (6 B.C. – A.D. 30)

Biblical	Secular
6/5 B.C. Mary gives birth to Jesus the Messiah A.D. 7–8 Jesus in the temple at age 12 26 Jesus begins ministry 30 Jesus' crucifixion, resurrection, and ascension	37–4 B.C. Herod the Great 27 B.C.–A.D. 14 Emperor Augustus 20 B.C. Herod's temple begun 6 B.C. Census ordered by Quirinius, governor of Syria A.D. 14–37 Emperor Tiberius 18 Caiaphas anointed as high priest 26 Pilate appointed procurator over Judea 26–27 Ministry of John the Baptist

Jesus. Born of a virgin; descendant of David and Adam; God in human form; the Word made flesh; the Son of God; the hero of *The Story*; name is the Greek form of Joshua, "the Lord is salvation"; *Christ* is the Greek equivalent of the Hebrew *Messiah*, which means "anointed," indicating Christ's kingship.

Joseph. Husband of Mary; when assured by God that Mary's child was God's, he protected her from public shame and joined in the adventure of raising God's Son; name means "may God add."

Magi. Probably from Persia or southern Arabia; devoted to astrology, divination, and interpreting dreams; visited the baby Jesus.

Mary. Wife of Joseph; mother of Jesus; a willing participant in God's plan of salvation; name is a form of Miriam, meaning "loved by God."

Quirinius. Roman governor of Syria when Joseph and Mary were summoned to Bethlehem for census.

Simeon. A devout Jew; met baby Jesus when he was brought by Mary and Joseph for his presentation in the temple; name means "he hears."

Chapter Overview

He walked with Adam and Eve in the garden. He spoke to Moses in the fire of a burning bush. He guided Israel in a cloud by day and fire by night. He sat enthroned over the ark of the covenant in the tabernacle and temple. But all of these were just the warm-up for the main act of the story. Now, the Lord would come himself, fully man and fully God.

The manner of his coming could not have been more amazing or unlikely. The Creator of the universe developed from a tiny embryo, to fetus, to newborn baby, passing through the birth canal and taking his first breath in the smelly air of an animal stable. His mother and his adopted father welcomed him with joy and trepidation.

The doctrine of the incarnation — the eter-

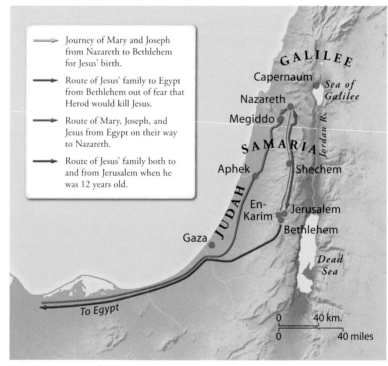

Journey of Mary and Joseph from Nazareth to Bethlehem for Jesus' birth.

Route of Jesus' family to Egypt from Bethlehem out of fear that Herod would kill Jesus.

Route of Mary, Joseph, and Jesus from Egypt on their way to Nazareth.

Route of Jesus' family both to and from Jerusalem when he was 12 years old.

GALILEE · Capernaum · Sea of Galilee · Nazareth · Megiddo · Jordan R. · SAMARIA · Aphek · Shechem · JUDAH · En-Karim · Jerusalem · Bethlehem · Gaza · Dead Sea · To Egypt · 0 40 km. · 0 40 miles

The early years of Jesus.

nal God entering the limitations of time and space and being born as a human being — this doctrine lies at the heart of the Christian faith. While every other religion welcomes moral teachers and angelic messengers, we worship the God-man. In what can only be described as a mind-bending mystery, the child born in a manger and known to us as Jesus Christ is one person with two natures: fully human, fully divine. While the many things Jesus said revealed God in a way no other words could, it was the Word himself who was the fullest revelation. As Paul wrote, "The Son is the image of the invisible God.... He is before all things, and in him all things hold together" (Col. 1:15 – 17).

In this chapter we see how God has arranged history and the events of the story to prepare for the coming of Jesus. Prophecies made centuries earlier were fulfilled. Angels made announcements. Shepherds touched the hem of eternity, and mighty kings shook in their boots. From this point forward, everyone would be asking one question, "Who is this man?"

Shepherds are the first to hear the good news of Jesus' birth.

Section Commentary

The Word (John 1)

In his introduction, John took great care to explain exactly who Jesus is — "the Word was God." Commentators often mention that "the Word" (Greek *logos*) was a popular philosophical concept for the readers John targeted with his gospel. These commentators suggest John was describing Jesus as the fulfillment of their philosophical intuitions and intellectual longings. Our words come from us — from our minds and the air we expire — communicating who we are. Our words express our identity. Identifying Jesus as "the Word" of God, who *was* God and was eternally *with* God, is equivalent to calling Jesus "God."

John also wanted us to see that the coming of the Word, Jesus Christ, is part of the larger story. John made a comparison in his opening verses between God's creative action at the beginning of the story of Scripture (see Genesis 1) and the creative act we witness in the next act of the story, the work that God's Son, the "Word" of God, did to save God's people from the tragic consequences of sin. John's point was clear: God himself has entered the story as a human being — and something new has happened, something we haven't seen since the beginning of time!

Jesus speaks with the teachers in the temple court at the age of twelve.

John wanted his readers to examine everything Jesus said and did in light of these opening verses. They frame the basic truth claim that, like light in a dark room, allows us to see the underlying significance of Jesus' words and deeds. At the same time, all the events John described are meant to prove the claim that John made in these opening verses.

According to Your Word (Luke 1)

It is interesting to compare Mary's response to God's call with the response of other figures in Scripture. Moses, for instance, was fright-ened and initially resistant to God's call. Samuel whispered, "Speak, LORD, for your servant is listening." Isaiah, his sins cleansed with fire from the altar, responded with a passionate, "Here am I. Send me!"

Mary was a model of courageous faith: "May your word to me be fulfilled." Her words express a willing submission to God's mysterious plan. She was not sure *how* God would do it, but she knew that she was willing to go where he directed.

Committed (Matthew 1)

Joseph and Mary were committed to each other. We learn that at the time of the angel's visit, they were betrothed. Although this was somewhat similar to our modern practice of being engaged, there were some differences. The couple was not yet officially married, in that they still lived apart and did not engage in sexual relations. Yet to have sexual relations with anyone else during betrothal would have been considered adultery, a transgression which carried the death penalty.

Joseph was also committed to obeying the Lord. Although God's call for his life was somewhat different from Mary's, it required the same step of faith. He had to trust and believe that, like her, God was at work doing something amazing. Even though it went against everything he understood about the world and had been taught, Joseph knew clearly that God had spoken to him, and he chose to obey.

To Bethlehem (Luke 2)

Throughout the story that has unfolded we have seen the sovereign hand of God moving nations to accomplish his will. God did this with Egypt when he called his people into freedom through Moses. He did it again with Babylon, using this pagan empire to send his people into exile. And God did it again with Persia, fulfilling his promise and returning his people back to the land of promise.

Each of these sovereign moments was leading up to the most important act of God thus far. At just the right time, the emperor of Rome was moved to call for a census. This call brought Joseph and his very pregnant wife to Bethlehem, the prophesied city of the Messiah. The prophecy that the Messiah, the promised descendant of David, would be born in Bethlehem was being fulfilled by the sovereign hand of God.

Movements (Matthew 2)

Even if the Jews were slow to remember it, the Old Testament prophets had clearly told Israel that God was going to bring people from all the nations into his covenant family. From the beginning, God promised Abraham that his offspring (literally, his "seed") would be a blessing to the nations. Matthew picks up on this theme by highlighting the visit of the magi, stargazers from the East. We are reminded that the coming of God's Son, Jesus, had universal implications. God was already at work, bringing outsiders from distant lands to meet his saving Son.

God the Father also used Joseph to save his Son from the wrath of Herod the Great, a notoriously violent king. When Herod learned from the magi that the prophesied Messiah had recently been born, he, like Pharaoh many centuries before, had all the male children of Bethlehem killed. But he was too late to stop God's plans from unfolding — the holy family was already on its way to Egypt.

His Father's House (Luke 2)

We do not know how soon Jesus, in his humanity, was fully aware of his divinity. Unlike a modern biography, the gospel writers arranged their story about Jesus with an eye on the theological significance of his life, so they made no attempt to capture and record each and every event of Jesus' childhood and adolescence. We don't have detailed stories or additional insight into the early years of Jesus, but at the same time, we can be sure that every detail of each writer's story has been told to tell us something important. Clearly, Luke selected this story for a reason. He wanted us to understand that by the age of twelve Jesus had a theologically advanced mind — and he knew who his real Father was.

Discussion Questions

1. The gospel writers were concerned with deepening their readers' theological understanding of Jesus. We can see this especially in John. Do you find yourself drawn to or repelled by theological inquiry? Explain.

2. If someone asked you to explain why you believe that Jesus is both fully man and fully God, how would you draw on these passages to do that?

23

JESUS' MINISTRY BEGINS

Plot Points

- Jesus' ministry was announced and endorsed by John the Baptist, one of the most significant figures in Judea at that time.
- The four evangelists emphasized not only Jesus' message, miracles, and atoning death, but how he lived his life in full accordance with God's will, the life we were meant to live.
- Jesus' message was authenticated with miracles.
- The primary opposition to Jesus' ministry (and that of John before him) came from the religious leaders of the day.

Unique Passages

Each of the gospel writers sought to present a distinct portrait of Jesus Christ. He selected certain events and not others to highlight a specific truth about Christ's identity and mission. This chart lists some of the passages unique to each author.

Gospel	Events and Teachings
Matthew	Angel's explanation to Joseph of circumstances surrounding Jesus' birth
	Visit of magi to Jesus
	Flight to Egypt and home in Nazareth
	Jesus' woes on Chorazin and Bethsaida for failing to repent
	Unique parables: the weeds and tares, the hidden treasure, the valuable pearl, the dragnet, the house owner
	Jesus' teaching on how to treat and forgive a sinful brother or sister
	Judgment at Jesus' coming
	Judas's guilt and suicide
	Stone rolled away at the resurrection
	Report of soldiers who guarded the tomb to Jewish authorities
	Appearance of risen Jesus to the Eleven in Galilee

Gospel	Events and Teachings
Mark	Parable of the seeds' spontaneous growth
	Jesus' healing of blind man at Bethsaida
Luke	John's birth foretold to Zechariah
	Mary's visit to Elizabeth and the Magnificat
	John's growth and early life
	Birth of Jesus and announcement to the shepherds
	Jesus' circumcision and presentation at the temple
	Jesus' first Passover in Jerusalem
	Jesus' ministry and rejection at Nazareth
	Jesus' raising of the widow's son at Nain
	Jesus' sending out of the Seventy
	Jesus' visit with Mary and Martha
	Jesus' healing of ten lepers while traveling through Samaria and Galilee
	Jesus' appearance on the road to Emmaus
John	The preincarnate Word
	Identification of Jesus as the Son of God by John the Baptist
	Jesus' first followers
	Jesus' turning of water into wine
	Jesus' first cleansing of the temple at Passover
	Interviewing of Jesus by Nicodemus, a Pharisee
	Jesus' discussion with the Samaritan woman
	Jesus' healing of a lame man in Jerusalem on the Sabbath
	Jesus' teaching on his equality with the Father
	Jesus' teaching that he is the "true bread," followed by many disciples leaving
	Jesus' teaching that he is the Light of the World
	Jesus' claim to have existed before Abraham
	Two attempts to arrest Jesus for blasphemy
	Jesus' raising of Lazarus from the dead
	Request of Greeks to meet Jesus
	Jesus' washing of the disciples' feet
	Many unique teachings in the upper room
	Jesus' postresurrection appearance to Mary Magdalene
	Jesus' postresurrection appearance to disciples while fishing

For a complete list, see Robert L. Thomas, *Charts of the Gospels and the Life of Christ*, 36 – 42.

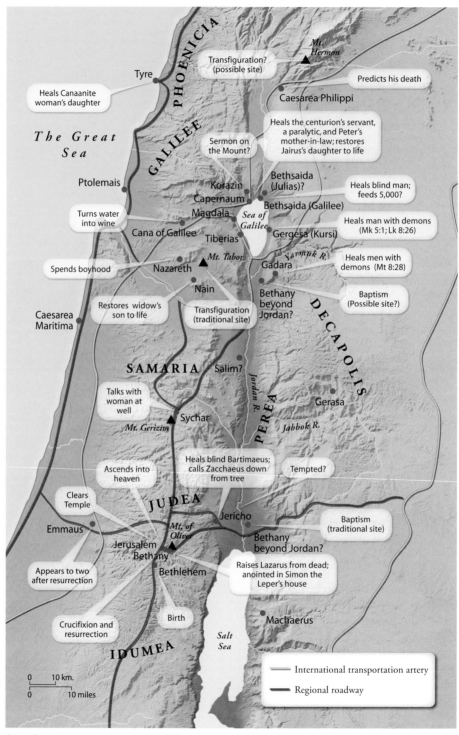

Jesus' ministry.

Cast of Characters

Andrew. One of Jesus' twelve apostles; brother of Simon Peter; the first of the disciples; left his fishing trade to follow Jesus; name means "manly."

Bartholomew. One of Jesus' twelve apostles; may have been Nathanael (mentioned in John's gospel); name means "son of Talmai."

Elizabeth. Mother of John the Baptist; name means "God is my oath."

Herod Antipas. Son of Herod the Great; ruled in Galilee; married the wife of his half brother, Herod Philip; murdered John the Baptist; was part of Jesus' trial; eventually died in exile.

Herod the Great. King of Judea when Jesus was born; a murderous ruler who posed as a Jewish king; built the temple Jesus worshiped in; name means "heroic."

James. Son of Alphaeus; one of Jesus' twelve apostles; Jesus' brother or near relative; witness to the resurrection; author of the New Testament letter of James.

James. Son of Zebedee; one of Jesus' twelve apostles; brother of John; left his work as a fisherman to follow Jesus; part of Jesus' inner circle; name a form of "Jacob."

Jesus. Born of a virgin; descendant of David and Adam; God in human form; the Son of God; the hero of *The Story*; name is the Greek form of Joshua, "the Lord is salvation"; *Christ* is the Greek equivalent of the Hebrew *Messiah*, which means "anointed," indicating Christ's kingship; has frequent run-ins with demons, disease, and religious leaders.

Joanna. Wife of Chuza; one of the female disciples who helped fund Jesus' ministry; witnessed the empty tomb.

John. Son of Zebedee; one of Jesus' twelve apostles; brother of James; believed to be "the beloved disciple"; author of the gospel that bears his name, three epistles, and the apocalyptic book that closes the canon; banished to the Isle of Patmos; died in Ephesus having lived more than ninety years; name means "the Lord is gracious."

John the Baptist. Son of Zechariah and Elizabeth; the forerunner of Jesus, preparing the way for the Messiah; fearless prophet; murdered by Herod Antipas; name means "the Lord is gracious."

Judas Iscariot. One of Jesus' twelve apostles; eventually betrayed Jesus to trial and death; Iscariot probably means "man of Kerioth," a village in the tribe of Judah.

Mary. Mother of James and Joseph; sister of Mary the mother of Jesus; wife of Cleopas; name means "loved by God."

Mary. Sister of Martha and Lazarus; sat at Jesus' feet and learned from him; name means "loved by God."

Mary Magdalene. Delivered from demons by Jesus; first witness to the resurrected Jesus; name means "loved by God."

Matthew. One of Jesus' twelve apostles; a former tax collector called to follow Jesus; author of the gospel that bears his name; also called Levi; name means "gift of the Lord."

Nathanael. See "Bartholomew."

Nicodemus. A Pharisee who visited Jesus in the night, probably to hide his association; asked penetrating questions and received revealing answers; eventually proclaimed his commitment to Christ publicly, assisting in Jesus' burial; name means "conqueror of the people."

Peter. One of Jesus' twelve apostles; a leader among Jesus' inner circle and in the early church; a man of bold proclamations; humbled by his own failures but restored by Jesus' grace; author of two epistles; originally named Simon; called Cephas, Aramaic form of "rock," by Jesus; name is Greek for "rock."

Pharisees. From an Aramaic word signifying "to separate"; originated in the second half of the second century B.C.; focused on strict legal observance; stressed the external, formal, and mechanical adherence at the expense of true righteousness.

Philip. One of Jesus' twelve apostles; from Bethsaida, the same city as Andrew and Peter; name means "lover of horses."

Sadducees. Greek form of the Hebrew *zaddukim*, derived from Zadok, said to have founded the sect; aristocratic and politically conservative; doctrinally opposed to the teaching of the Pharisees; denied the resurrection.

Samaritan woman. Unnamed woman who conversed with Jesus; received one of Jesus' most straightforward statements of self-disclosure in the Gospels; experienced a radical conversion and led others to Jesus.

Simon the Zealot. One of Jesus' twelve apostles; probably a member of a fanatical sect of Zealots before following Jesus; name means "hearing."

Susanna. One of the female disciples who helped fund Jesus' ministry.

Thaddaeus. One of Jesus' twelve apostles; also called Judas; name means "praise."

Thomas. One of Jesus' twelve apostles; asked hard questions and looked for solid answers; sometimes lacked faith; also called "Didymus" ("twin"); name means "twin."

Chapter Overview

In the closing verses of his gospel, John commented that it would be impossible to write down everything Jesus said and did. In other words, the gospel writers have done more than present the eyewitness testimonies of the life of Jesus in written form. The details of his life and ministry have been selected and arranged to communicate something specific and significant.

Each of the four Gospels has a distinct contribution to make to our understanding of Jesus. Matthew wrote to emphasize Jesus as *King*. For instance, unlike Luke who traced Jesus' lineage back to Adam, Matthew traced his line to David. As we have already seen, God's great promise to David was that his descendant would be established on an eternal throne. Matthew was making an important claim: Jesus is that King!

Mark emphasized that Jesus was a *servant*. Unlike Matthew and Luke, Mark included no genealogy for Jesus. Why? Because a servant's ancestors were not important. We see that the Holy Spirit "sent [Jesus] out of the wilderness." Jesus into the desert. In other words, Jesus is humbly going about the business of his Father.

Luke placed a great emphasis on Jesus as *man*. As noted already, he traces Jesus' lineage back to Adam, highlighting Jesus' common bond to all people. Luke spent special time emphasizing Mary's pregnancy. He tied Jesus' birth to events in history. He showed Jesus being presented as a newborn baby in the temple, just like every other child in Israel.

John placed special emphasis on Jesus as

God. He traced Jesus' lineage to the eternal, second person of the Trinity, the Word. He is "God…the one and only" (1:18). John recorded the many times that Jesus identified himself closely with the Father, making himself equal with God. He also emphasized the times Jesus spoke of his preexistence in eternity.

The Story weaves together these various messages into one narrative. In doing so, we are able to grasp the

Jesus with the Samaritan woman at the well.

Manuel Panselinos/Wikimedia Commons

unified message of the four evangelists. It is also important, however, to recognize that the Holy Spirit inspired four distinct perspectives on Jesus. Each one is a self-contained revelation of our Lord, written for a unique purpose.

Section Commentary

John and Jesus (Matthew 3, John 1 – 2)

According to Luke, John the Baptist and Jesus were cousins. Prophecies had foretold the coming of each one. And each of them was called into public ministry. John's work was that of forerunner. He passionately prepared the ground for the one who would come after him. John must have been surrounded by people who wanted to make *him* the point of his ministry. But he would have none of it. When Jesus arrived on the scene, John was clear that Jesus was the one he had been waiting for, proclaiming, "Look, the Lamb of God."

According to John's gospel, John the Baptist also helped direct some of Jesus' first disciples to him. John willingly encouraged his own disciples to follow Jesus. Andrew, Simon Peter, Philip, and Nathanael (i.e., Bartholomew) were added to Jesus' company as a result of John's witness.

Tempted (Matthew 4)

As Jesus of Nazareth, God willingly stepped into the full range of human experience. Jesus grew tired and needed sleep. He hungered and thirsted. And he was tempted to sin, just like we are — with one important difference: Jesus never gave in to temptation and sinned. Consider the temptation account in light of Hebrews 4:14 – 16:

Therefore, since we have a great high priest who has ascended into heaven, Jesus the Son of God, let us hold firmly to the faith we profess. For we do not have a high priest who is unable to empathize with our weaknesses, but we have one who has been tempted in every way, just as we are — yet he did not sin. Let us then approach God's throne of grace with confidence, so that we may receive mercy and find grace to help us in our time of need.

The Inside Story (John 3 – 4)

It is interesting to compare the stories of Nicodemus and the Samaritan woman. On the one hand, we have two very different people. Nicodemus was a Pharisee and a member of the Sanhedrin. He had been trained theologically and could probably discuss fine points of the law with the best scholars of his day. In other words, he was the ultimate "insider." The woman at the well, however, was a Samaritan, five times divorced, and was living with a man who was not her husband. She was, by every measure, an "outsider." Nicodemus and the Samaritan woman also contrast in how they came to meet Jesus. Nicodemus sought him out. The woman at the well bumped into him by accident. Each of them also met Jesus at unusual times. The Samaritan woman came to the well in the middle of the day, when it would certainly have been deserted. Nicodemus came to Jesus in the dark of night, when no one would recognize him. The woman bore the shame of her lifestyle. Nicodemus was trying to preserve his reputation and avoid the shame of association with an upstart rabbi from Galilee.

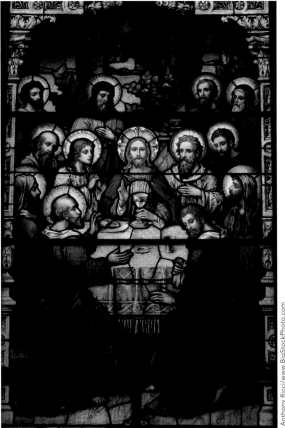

The disciples surround Jesus at the Last Supper.

© Anthony Ricci/www.BigStockPhoto.com

Despite these differences, there is a striking similarity between the two: in his dialogue with each person, Jesus spoke with unusual candor about who he was. In both cases Jesus claimed that he was the secret to eternal life. With Nicodemus, he drew on an Old Testament image a law expert would grasp immediately, identifying himself with the bronze serpent that brought healing in the wilderness. Jesus stressed that truth by claiming that everyone who believes may have eternal life in him. Jesus shared with the woman, "Whoever drinks the water I give them will never thirst. Indeed, the water I give them will become in them a spring of water welling up to eternal life" (4:14). John arranged these stories intentionally. His aim was to show us that it does not matter if one is at the top or the bottom of the social, religious, or economic ladder; Jesus is the only way to life.

Power (Matthew 4; Mark 1–3)

Throughout the Enlightenment, culminating near the turn of the twentieth century, theological liberals worked hard to "demythologize" the Jesus story, removing stories that contain supernatural elements. They believed that the supernatural elements of the Gospels reflected the prescientific worldview of the authors and could be discarded. The real meaning of the stories was found in Jesus' message of love and peace.

But the *miracles* of Jesus cannot be separated from his *message*. Jesus' power ministry was inextricably wedded to his teaching ministry. Jesus' message of the kingdom was preached in sermons and in healing. Each time Jesus cast out demons, multiplied loaves, or miraculously raised someone from the dead, he was providing a signpost of the kingdom that had come, is coming, and will fully arrive when he returns to make all things new.

Disciples (Matthew 11; Mark 3; Luke 8)

Question: What was one of the most significant things Jesus did on earth? Answer: teach and disciple twelve men to carry the gospel to all people. Something becomes clear when we observe Jesus' life closely: In his public ministry, he was always teaching at two levels. Every time he interacted with a crowd or with an individual, Jesus was ministering to those people, but he was also *teaching his disciples*. Take some time and study how often Jesus does or says something to a crowd and then processes it with his team! Consider how many different ways he does something and then turns to them and says, "Now you do it." Jesus was imparting his life into the apostles every step along the journey.

Discussion Questions

1. What role did John the Baptist play in Jesus' life and ministry? What can we learn from John about what it means to be a Christian witness?

2. Jesus chose to be baptized and then experienced temptation in the desert. Why do you think these things had to happen in his life?

3. John the Baptist and Jesus frequently had conflict with the religious leaders. What issues characterized these conflicts? What lessons should we draw from these encounters?

24

Plot Points

- Jesus, preaching in parables, calls out those who have ears to hear.
- Jesus confronts the religious leaders, calling their external expression of obedience to account for their internal lack of compassion.
- In the Sermon on the Mount, Jesus announces the "constitution" of his kingdom.
- Jesus demonstrates his power over the forces of chaos — stormy seas, sickness, and even death.

"I Am"

Statement and Reference	Significance	Old Testament Background
"I, the one speaking to you — I am he" (4:26).	Jesus reveals His identity as the Messiah to the Samaritan woman.	Dt. 18:15–22; Isa. 9:6–7; 11:1–10; 28:16; 53; Jer. 23:5–6; Mal. 4
"I am the bread of life" (6:25–59).	Jesus identifies the divine origin and life-giving power of the wilderness manna with Himself.	Exod. 16:31–36; Dt. 8:3; Neh. 9:16–21; Ps. 78:21–25
"I am the light of the world" (8:12–20; 9:1–7).	Throughout the OT, light is a symbol not only of truth and righteousness, but the Lord's presence.	Gen. 1:3–5; Exod. 13:21–22; 2 Sam. 23:1–5a; Pss. 4:6; 27:1; 89:15; 90:8; 118:27; Isa. 9:2
"Before Abraham was born, I am" (8:52–59).	Jesus indicates His pre-existence as a member of the Trinity.	Gen. 14:18–20, 21:12; Exod. 3:13–14
"I am the gate for the sheep" (10:1–10).	The sheepfold door both allowed entrance and prevented trespass; Jesus will be a door for His sheep.	Jer. 23:1–3

Cast of Characters

Daughter of Herodias. Unnamed character; called Salome by Josephus; danced for Herod Antipas, her father's half brother, and his guests and granted one request; asked for the head of John the Baptist.

Herod Antipas. Ruled in Galilee; married the wife of his half brother, Herod Philip; murdered John the Baptist; was part of Jesus' trial; eventually died in exile.

Herodias. Wife of Herod Antipas; formerly married to Philip; daughter of a ruler; politically engaged.

Jairus. A synagogue leader whose young daughter was raised from the dead by Jesus; name means "he will enlighten."

Jesus. See previous chapter.

Legion. Demonic entity cast out of a person and into a herd of pigs.

Little daughter. Unnamed daughter of Jairus; raised from the dead by Jesus.

Statement and Reference	Significance	Old Testament Background
"I am the good shepherd" (10:11–18).	Running through Israel's historical, prophetic, wisdom, and poetic literature is a powerful image: God as Shepherd. He is prefigured imperfectly in David's reign. His unfaithful representatives—prophets, priests, and kings—are forever superseded when he comes himself in Jesus.	Gen. 48:14–15; Num. 27:15–17; 2 Sam. 5:1–3; Pss. 23:1–6; 80:1; Isa. 40:10–11; Jer. 31:10–11; Ezek. 34:22–24; 37:24; Mic. 5:1–4
"I am God's Son" (10:32–36).	In Jewish culture, sons followed in their fathers' footsteps; sonship indicated representation; the Father shown forth in the face of the Son.	Ps. 82:6
"The Father is in me and I in the Father" (10:32–38; 14:10–11).	Jesus indicates his intimate relationship with God the Father can be shared with his followers, far surpassing the OT experience.	Ps. 82:6
"I am the resurrection and the life" (11:21–27).	Though only hinted at in the OT, Jesus explicitly holds out the promise of resurrection first in raising Lazarus and ultimately on Easter morning.	Ps. 16:10–11; Ezek. 37:11–14
"I am the way and the truth and the life" (14:5–6).	Throughout the OT, the "way of righteousness" is commended to Israel. Jesus himself became our pathway to a new, abundant and everlasting life.	Jos. 24:16–18; Ps. 16:11; Isa. 30:19–2?; 40:3; Jer. 21:8–10, 50:5; Mal. 3:1
"I am the true vine" (15:1–5).	The vine Israel was meant to be, Jesus is; he holds out the offer for each of us to join with him in representing the Father's intentions to the world around us.	Ps. 80:8–19; Isa. 5:1–7; Jer. 2:21; 12:7–10; Ezek. 19:10–14; Hos. 10:1; Jl 1:7

Prepared by Adam T. Barr

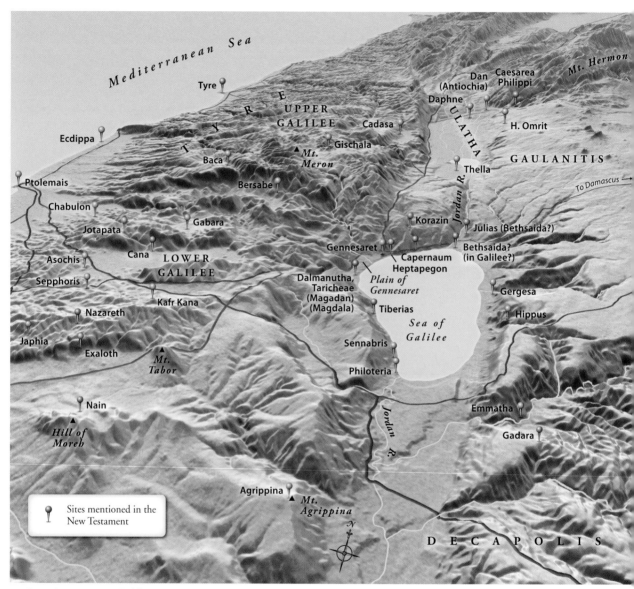

Jesus' ministry in Galilee.

Man with evil spirit. Unnamed character; delivered from demonic possession by a demonic entity named Legion; freed from life among the tombs to a life of witness.

Peter. One of Jesus' twelve apostles; a leader among Jesus' inner circle and in the early church; a man of bold proclamations and actions; for instance, walking on water and confessing Jesus as Messiah.

Pharisees. See previous chapter.

Two blind men. Unnamed characters healed by Jesus; called Jesus "Son of David," an indication of his royal lineage.

Woman of great faith. Unnamed character; suffered from constant bleeding for many years; healed when, in faith, she touched the hem of Jesus' robe; commended for her faith.

Chapter Overview

Jesus' ministry was composed of several different but complementary elements. He was always preaching, and his messages were often communicated through parables. These stories were more than simple illustrations designed to make his teaching more understandable to his listeners. In fact, the parables that Jesus told were often designed to *conceal* the truth they carried from those who were not seeking the truth. In addition to his parables, Jesus also communicated in more straightforward, easily understood ways, as we see in his Sermon on the Mount. Regardless of his style and method, his messages were always in some way about the kingdom of God.

Jesus' ministry was also infused with miracles. The miracles of Jesus were a confirmation of his message, and each miracle was also

a message in itself. His miracles were signposts directing the attention of those watching to the great day when all things will be made new. The miracles were also testimonies to Jesus' identity. For instance, when Jesus sat on a hillside and fed a multitude with five loaves and two fish, he demonstrated the kind of King he was and challenged people to seek the true bread that would satisfy their spiritual hunger, himself.

As observed in the preceding chapter, Jesus' relationship with his disciples was at the heart of his ministry. In particular, the twelve apostles were a central focus for his work. Jesus took time out from his public ministry to explain his more difficult sayings to his disciples. He traveled and spent time with these disciples, and he devoted his three years of earthly ministry to sharing his day-to-day life with them. Ultimately, he was preparing them to "catch" his life and pass it on to others.

Section Commentary

The Parables (Mark 4; Luke 10, 15)

Often today we place a high value on being clear and straightforward in our communication. We appreciate speech that is transparent, in which the meaning is immediately apparent to the listener. A good communicator will make it easy for anyone to follow his or her line of argument from opening to close. And we especially appreciate it when speakers take the time to make their message attractive and shape it to the interest of the audience. Marketers spend millions of dollars each year producing commercials to do just that — communicate their message in a way that grabs our attention.

The points of Jesus' sermons were plainly spoken, but they were not always obvious. In

David Bivin/www.LifeintheHolyLand.com

The Sea of Galilee, on which the disciples were sailing when Jesus calmed the storm.

fact, the more time you devote to studying them, the more amazed you become at the depth and nuance in his stories. Jesus did not try to craft messages for "one-ear," casual listeners. Instead, he preached "lean forward in your seats" sermons that sifted out the true listeners from those with a passing interest in his messages. Those who lacked an interest in the truth or the heart of humility needed to listen and learn often missed the point of his messages. But those who took the time to listen and ask questions soon discovered that the teaching of Jesus was like nothing they had ever heard before (Mark 1:22).

Life in the Kingdom (Matthew 5 – 7)

Jesus did not come to show us an easier way to live. His impatience with the religious leaders of his day was that they believed that following an elaborate system of rules would make them right with God rather than seeking to follow God's commandments with a sincere heart. As we read the Sermon on the Mount, one thing is obvious: Jesus' message of the kingdom was so perfect, pure, high, and holy that *no one* could consistently live it out. And that's why he had come, to live the perfect life we could not and to give us an example that we could follow — while trusting him to make us right with God.

To the Other Side (Mark 4 – 5)

The stories of Jesus calming the storm and casting Legion from the man in the region of the Gerasenes have a common emphasis: Jesus' divine power over the forces of chaos. The story of the demoniac demonstrates Jesus' decisive control over Satan's minions. They recognize him as the Son of God and must answer to him.

The story of the stormy sea opens up even more interesting territory. In the Jewish worldview, the stormy sea harkened back to the floodwaters of Noah's day and the chaotic waters of Creation. Storms and squalls spoke of that chaos again. But this story is about more than Jesus mastering a storm. In a subtle way, Mark is showing us that Jesus is the great "I AM" — Yahweh come in the flesh.

Mark is clearly encouraging the reader to answer the question the disciples ask, "Who is this? Even the wind and the waves obey him!" (4:41). For anyone conversant with the Old Testament, there was only one answer: Yahweh, the God of Israel, who demonstrates his might by mastering the waves.

> "Who shut up the sea behind doors …
> when I said, 'This far you may come and
>   no farther;
>   here is where your proud waves halt'?"
> — Job 38:8, 11

> You answer us with awesome and righteous
>   deeds,
>   God our Savior,
> the hope of all the ends of the earth
>   and of the farthest seas,
> who formed the mountains by your power,
>   having armed yourself with strength,
> who stilled the roaring of the seas,
>   the roaring of their waves,

> and the turmoil of the nations.
> — Psalm 65:5 – 7

> Who is like you, LORD God Almighty?
>   You, LORD, are mighty, and your
>   faithfulness surrounds you.
> You rule over the surging sea;
>   when its waves mount up, you still them.
> — Psalm 89:8 – 9

> He stilled the storm to a whisper;
>   the waves of the sea were hushed.
> They were glad when it grew calm,
>   and he guided them to their desired haven.
> — Psalm 107:29 – 30

Who is this man, who commands the wind and waves and demonstrates authority over demonic powers? That's the question Mark wants us to ask as well.

Two Ways to Rule
(Matthew 9; Mark 5 – 6)

In this series of encounters, we see two kings in action. One wears a crown and purple robes. He takes what he wants and rubs elbows with the emperor. Herod Antipas was a notorious ruler who had an affair with his brother's wife and arrested and executed John the Baptist. Without a doubt, Herod believed he was somebody important and wielded his power to prove it.

But another king is also highlighted in these passages. He does not have a place to lay his head. He survives on the generosity of others, and he makes his place with the lowly. For this king, power is compassion extended to bring healing to others. We see this in his healing the blind, a bleeding woman, and a dead little girl. Jesus was a different kind of king.

"It Is I" (Matthew 14)

The encounter in this passage further emphasizes Jesus' divinity. When the disciples say, "It's a ghost," the Lord replies, in the most literal sense, "It is I," an allusion to the name of God (Yahweh), revealed to Moses at the burning bush.

Jesus claimed to be the Bread of Life.

The Bread of Life (John 6)

Jesus had a habit of speaking the truth. And his habit of speaking the truth was shocking to people unaccustomed to it. But most shocking of all are the claims that Jesus made about himself, claims that were bound to offend people:

People believed him to be a rabbi. But unlike other teachers of his day, he claimed that faith in *him* was just as important as faith in his teachings.

People thought he was a miracle worker who could make bread multiply and feed the starving masses. But Jesus also claimed to be the "bread of life," the one person who could satisfy our spiritual hunger.

People were looking for a person who could provide practical instruction and help them obey the requirements of God's Law. But Jesus claimed that it was only by consuming his flesh and blood that they would have life at all. His statements confused and upset his listeners, but one thing was evident to all: Jesus claimed to be more than just a teacher; he saw himself as the one person who could meet our spiritual needs and make us right with God.

Discussion Questions

1. What are some of the dangers in trying to make the message of Jesus easier for people to understand? On the other hand, how can we avoid making it too complicated?

2. What are some of the dangers in not working to contextualize the gospel in our ministry setting? How does Jesus help us do this?

JESUS, THE SON OF GOD

25

Plot Points

- A massive showdown with the religious leaders seems inevitable.
- Jesus, once again, is affirmed as God's Son by God himself as he speaks with Moses and Elijah on a mountaintop.
- The question of Jesus' identity is emerging as the central concern of Jesus' day and of the Gospels.
- The disciples, despite Jesus' frank proclamations, still do not understand that he will die and be raised again in three days.
- Jesus raises a man three days dead, demonstrating that he is the resurrection and the life.
- The conspiracy to kill Jesus is set in motion with the recruitment of Judas Iscariot.

Jesus (6 B.C. – A.D. 30)

Biblical	Secular
A.D. 7–8 Jesus in the temple at age 12 26 Jesus begins ministry 30 Jesus' crucifixion, resurrection, and ascension	4 B.C.–A.D. 6 Herod Archelaus 4 B.C.–A.D. 34 Herod Philip II 4 B.C.–A.D. 39 Herod Antipas A.D. 14–37 Emperor Tiberius 26–18 Caiaphas anointed as high priest 26–26 Pilate appointed procurator over Judea 26–27 Ministry of John the Baptist

Cast of Characters

Caiaphas. High priest during Jesus' trial before the Sanhedrin; unwittingly prophesied that Jesus would die for the nation; name means "depression."

Elijah. Important prophet of Judah during the time of Ahab; associated with the coming of the Messiah.

James. Son of Zebedee; one of Jesus' twelve apostles; brother of John; left his work as a fisherman to follow Jesus; part of Jesus' inner circle; witness to the transfiguration; name a form of Jacob.

Jesus. See chapter 23.

John. Son of Zebedee; one of Jesus' twelve apostles; brother of James; believed to be "the beloved disciple"; witness to the transfiguration; name means "the Lord is gracious."

Lazarus. Brother of Mary and Martha; a wealthy man; a friend of Jesus; died and was resurrected by Jesus.

Martha. Sister of Mary and Lazarus; liked to work hard, sometimes at the expense of missing out on learning from Jesus; name means "lady."

Mary. Sister of Martha and Lazarus; sat at Jesus' feet and learned from him; name means "loved by God."

Moses. Leader and lawgiver of Israel in the exodus and great desert journey.

Peter. See previous chapter.

Rich young man. Unnamed character; man of great possessions and personal discipline; found the price of following Jesus too steep.

Satan. A spiritual being opposed to Jesus' ministry; influenced Judas in his betrayal of Jesus.

Thomas. One of Jesus' twelve apostles; asked hard questions and looked for solid answers; sometimes lacked faith; challenged his fellow apostles to be willing to die with Jesus; also called Didymus ("twin"); name means "twin."

Chapter Overview

Each of the Gospels gifts us with a biography of Jesus, sharing the things he did and said. However, the central point of each gospel is not simply to convey information about what Jesus did and said. Each gospel is written to bring the reader to grips with who Jesus *is*.

The Gospels, especially the first three (called Synoptics), take time to "drop hints" along the way. Each is written to force the reader to scratch his or her head and wonder, *Who is this man?* They do this by allowing us to see Jesus through several perspectives. Sometimes we are with the disciples, wondering what Jesus could possibly mean. Sometimes we are with a needy person, coming to Jesus for help. Sometimes we are meant to see ourselves in the less favorable characters too!

As Jesus moves closer to the cross, the question of his identity takes on more urgency. The disciples are beginning to make statements about him. The crowds are wondering. The religious leaders are furious that Jesus himself is making statements such as, "Before Abraham was born, I am!" For them, that sounded suspiciously like Jesus was calling himself the "I AM" who spoke from the burning bush on Sinai. It is becoming clearer and clearer that Jesus will not allow people simply to call him a good teacher.

Section Commentary

The Son Confessed and Revealed
(Matthew 17; Mark 8 – 9; Luke 9)

Peter's confession, "You are the Messiah," represents the high-water mark in the history of human understanding up to that point. In those four words, Peter articulated the hope of the ages. For the first time in human history, God's prophesied Anointed One was clearly recognized.

But full understanding of Jesus' identity and mission was still lacking. Peter, one of his closest friends and disciples, still did not grasp the magnitude of his own confession of faith. Although Peter rightly identified Jesus as the fulfillment of the Old Testament prophecies, another question remained: Did Peter understand the totality of what the Messiah was meant to do? The Old Testament prophecies contained two strains of teaching on the Messiah. One thread emphasized the Messiah's triumphant rule, ushering in a new Israel. The other spoke of suffering and death. When Peter attempted to reject this latter aspect of the Messiah, Jesus quickly and forcefully rebuked him.

Peter's confession is complemented and undergirded by a much higher authority. Jesus is transfigured, and on the mountaintop he appears in all his glorious splendor. As at Jesus' baptism, the Father again speaks his pleasure over the Son. Peter, James, and John look on as Moses and Elijah converse with the Messiah they had longed to see!

Radical Claims and Dangerous Opposition (John 7 – 8, 11)

Jesus' days were numbered. As his self-revelation became more explicit, his opposition grew more committed to silencing him. Many times Jesus had spoken of being "sent" from the Father. This kind of claim had remained open to interpretation, but when Jesus said, "Before Abraham was born, I am," he left the religious leaders with little doubt as to what he was saying. They knew that Jesus was claiming to be much more than a teacher.

The crowds were caught up in speculation as well. A buzz of questions grew up around Jesus. The issue increasingly boiled down to his identity: "Who is this man?" Standing before the tomb of Lazarus Jesus called out a man who had been dead for three days — a man whose

The tomb of Lazarus located in Bethany.

The Eastern Gate of Jerusalem, which Jesus passed through in his triumphal entry.

© William D. Mounce

body had already begun to decay, generating an unpleasant odor. While some may have claimed the little girl he raised from the dead was really "just sleeping," no one could doubt that Lazarus had been truly dead. The smell of death was unmistakable. Jesus demonstrated to all who were there that he had power and authority over the powers of death, disease, and demons.

A Matter of Faith (Mark 10; John 11)

Children understand dependence. They know what it means fully to trust another for all their needs. Sometimes, they do not even recognize they even have a need, because their needs are being met so well! For the rich young man who met Jesus, this kind of radical dependence on God seemed impossible. He lacked faith that God could meet his needs, and he rejected the invitation of Jesus, instead choosing to trust in his own wealth and resources. Many of us have two similar problems. We lack a true understanding of our real needs, having grown satisfied with the distractions of wealth the world provides. Even harder, though, is the decision we must make to transfer our trust — from faith in our own self-sufficiency to a radical dependence upon Jesus Christ to meet our needs. This heartfelt dependence lies at the heart of true faith, and it's the only appropriate response to the gospel.

Coming to a Head (Matthew 21; Mark 11 – 12, 14; Luke 22; John 12)

Most people would feel offended if a guest at a dinner party they were hosting suddenly got up, located a vacuum, and started cleaning. Their actions would carry a not-so-subtle implication: your home is a wreck, and I can do a better job of caring for it than you! The responsibilities — and rights — of a guest are very different than those of the home owner.

After allowing the crowds to greet him with shouts of "Hosanna!" Jesus entered the temple and did some housecleaning of his own. And he didn't enter as a guest; he asserted the rights an responsibilities of ownership. The religious leaders in the temple understood the clear message he was sending to them: "This place has been compromised, and I have the right to clean it." It was a message they did not want to hear.

Discussion Questions

1. C. S. Lewis commented, "You must make your choice. Either this man was, and is, the Son of God: or else a madman or something worse. You can shut him up for a fool, you can spit at him and kill him as a demon; or you can fall at his feet and call him Lord and God. But let us not come with any patronizing nonsense about his being a great human teacher. He has not left that open to us. He did not intend to." How does this chapter of the story substantiate this quote from Lewis?

2. Many Christians wear a bracelet embroidered with "W.W.J.D.?" — "What Would Jesus Do?" How does this question capture something important about Jesus? What does it miss?

26

THE HOUR OF DARKNESS

Plot Points

- In his last hours with his disciples, Jesus took time to teach them what true servanthood looks like and express his love for them, knowing they would abandon him.
- Even as he was arrested, Jesus was in control of the situation; he was not a victim but a champion on his way to battle.
- The religious and political leaders who crucified Jesus were motivated more by a desire for self-preservation than for justice.
- Jesus, fully man and fully God, felt the full weight of God's wrath against sin as he was beaten for our transgressions and lifted up on the cross for our healing.

The Passion Week

Day	Event	Reference
Sunday	Jesus enters Jerusalem on a donkey.	Matt. 21:1–17; Mark 11:1–11; Luke 19:29–44
Monday	Jesus curses the fig tree.	Matt. 21:18–19; Mark 11:12–14
	Jesus cleanses the temple.	Matt. 21:12–13; Mark 11:15–18; Luke 19:45–46
Tuesday	Jesus' authority is questioned.	Matt. 21:23–22:14; Mark 11:27–12:12; Luke 20:1–19
	Jesus teaches in the temple.	Matt. 22:41–46; Mark 12:35–37; Luke 20:41–44
	Mary anoints Jesus.	Matt. 26:6–13; Mark 14:3–9; John 12:2–8
Wednesday	Opponents form a plot to betray Jesus.	Matt. 26:14–16; Mark 14:10–11; Luke 22:3–6
Thursday	Jesus presides at the Last Supper.	Matt. 26:17–29; Mark 14:12–25; Luke 22:7–30
	Jesus prays in Gethsemane.	Matt. 26:30–46; Mark 14:26–42; Luke 22:39–46; John 18:1
Friday	Jesus is arrested and put on trial.	Matt. 26:47–27:26; Mark 14:43–15:15; Luke 22:47–23:25; John 18:2–19:16
	Jesus is crucified.	Matt. 27:31–56; Mark 15:20–46; Luke 23:26–49; John 19:16–30

Adapted from H. Wayne House, *Chronological and Background Charts of the New Testament*, 103.

Cast of Characters

Barabbas. A robber released by Pilate in exchange for Jesus' conviction.

Caiaphas. See previous chapter.

The centurion. Unnamed character; believed Jesus was the Son of God after seeing his death.

James. See previous chapter.

John. Son of Zebedee; one of Jesus' twelve apostles; brother of James; believed to be "the beloved disciple"; author of the gospel that bears his name, three epistles, and the apocalyptic book that closes the canon; banished to the Isle of Patmos; died in Ephesus having lived more than ninety years; name means "the Lord is gracious."

Judas Iscariot. One of Jesus' twelve apostles; eventually betrayed Jesus to trial and death; conscience-stricken, he returned

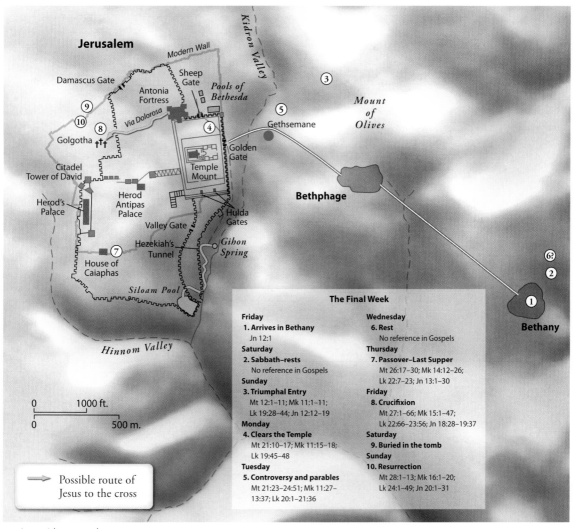

Jesus' last week.

his ill-gotten silver to the Sanhedrin, hung himself, and fell to a gruesome death.

Malchus. Servant of the high priest; ear struck off by Peter and healed by Jesus.

Mary. Mother of Jesus; present at the crucifixion; given into the care of John as Jesus died.

Mary. Wife of Clopas; Jesus' aunt; present at the crucifixion.

Mary Magdalene. Delivered of demons by Jesus; present at the crucifixion.

Peter. One of Jesus' twelve apostles; a leader among Jesus' inner circle; asked to pray with Jesus in the garden but slept instead; despite his promises, denied even knowing Jesus on the night of the Lord's arrest; restored to leadership after his repentance.

Philip. One of Jesus' twelve apostles; asked Jesus, "Show us the Father."

Pilate. Roman procurator of Judea; presided over Jesus' legal trial; attempted to evade a conviction while satisfying the Jewish leaders; eventually allowed a prisoner exchange, condemning Jesus and releasing Barabbas; name means "javelin carrier."

Simon. Father of Alexander and Rufus; forced to carry Jesus' cross; from Cyrene; perhaps one of the "men of Cyrene" who evangelized the Greeks (Acts 11:20); name means "he hears."

Thomas. One of Jesus' twelve apostles; asked hard questions and looked for solid answers; sometimes lacked faith; questioned how they could join Jesus if they did not know the way.

The two criminals. Unnamed characters; one hurled insults at Jesus; the other expressed faith and was promised a place in paradise.

Chapter Overview

When Jesus first began his public ministry, John the Baptist pointed at him and said, "Look, the Lamb of God!" During three years of ministry together, the disciples had come to believe Jesus was the promised Messiah. Although they believed he was the prophesied descendant of David destined to restore Israel, they were not prepared for the real-world application of his kingly crown. They were anticipating a golden circlet, not a mass of thorns.

Perhaps they began to comprehend that things would be different as he sat with them that night in the upper room? For several weeks

Courtesy of Mary Harrsch

The Chalice of Antioch. Some scholars believe a case can credibly be made that this cup, dating from the first century A.D., was designed to hold the original chalice used at the Last Supper.

Jesus had been quite clear about his mission: "[I] did not come to be served, but to serve, and to give [my] life as a ransom for many" (see Mark 10:45). As Jesus broke the bread and poured out the cup, calling the elements of the meal his body and blood, did they begin to understand what was about to happen?

We must not forget an important truth about the death of Jesus: he willingly walked to the cross. Jewish leaders may have worked the system and forced Pilate's hand, but the entire process was guided by the hand of God. From eternity this had been the plan, God's spotless Lamb slain for the sins of the world.

In recent decades it has become fashionable to portray Jesus as a victim of social injustice. Some have stated that Jesus was crushed under the thumb of the Roman Empire. Others have seen Jesus' suffering as a divine identification with victims everywhere. But that is not what Scripture says about Jesus' suffering.

The Bible tells us that Jesus was suffering under the wrath and punishment of God, not the corrupt injustice of Rome or the hatred of jealous Jewish leaders. Jesus drank the cup of *God's* judgment, not Pilate's. Jesus, in fact, became sin — identifying himself with our disobedience and rebellion against God — that we might become the righteousness of God!

The doctrine of substitutionary atonement is the belief that Christ willingly put himself in our place, suffering the penalty of our sin for us. This truth disarms every pretense of the religious perfectionist and undercuts any other formula for our salvation. For as we look at the horror of the cross, we realize something: the only reason God would do things this way is if there were no other way to save us.

Section Commentary

The Last Passover (Mark 14; John 13)

What exactly was the sequence of events on this night? How can the four Gospels be harmonized? The sequence of events probably ran like this:

1. Jesus washes the disciples' feet.
2. Jesus announces he will be betrayed.
3. Jesus hands the bread he has dipped to Judas, indicating he is the traitor.
4. Jesus institutes the Lord's Supper.

I Have Overcome the World (Matthew 26; John 14, 16–17)

Notice that Jesus viewed his ultimate victory as achieved already. Although he still had the suffering of the cross before him, Jesus had decisively determined his course of action. The knowledge of ultimate victory sustained him through his pain. Jesus knew he was going to die so that a new creation would begin, resurrected from the old. He knew that judgment would not only fall on him, but that his act of sacrifice would once and for all defeat the work of Satan.

In the Garden (Matthew 26, Luke 22, John 18)

Jesus prayed, "Father … take this cup from me." Context and common usage of this term make it easy for us to see that the "cup" signified the suffering Jesus was about to bear. But this phrase was more than a metaphor for his approaching ordeal. In the Old Testament, "the cup" was frequently a symbol of God's wrath. Consider these passages from the Old Testament Scriptures:

Awake, awake!
>Rise up, Jerusalem,
you who have drunk from the hand of
the LORD
>the cup of his wrath,
you who have drained to its dregs
>the goblet that makes people stagger.
>—Isaiah 51:17

This is what the LORD, the God of Israel, said to me: "Take from my hand this cup filled with the wine of my wrath and make all the nations to whom I send you drink it."
>—Jeremiah 25:15

The Trial (Matthew 26–27; Luke 22; John 18–19)

Jesus' trial followed this sequence:

1. Brought before Annas, the father-in-law of the high priest Caiaphas (John 18:12–14)
2. Brought into Caiaphas's house late in the night to stand before the Sanhedrin (Matt. 26:57–68; Mark 14:53–65; Luke 22:54–65; John 18:24)
3. Sentence ratified by the Sanhedrin early in the morning (Matt. 27:1; Mark 15:1; Luke 22:66–71)
4. Brought before Pilate (Matt. 27:2, 11–14; Mark 15:2–5; Luke 23:1–5; John 18:28–40)
5. Sent to Herod by Pilate because he is from Galilee (Luke 23:6–12)
6. Sent back to Pilate; scourged, sentenced, and handed over to be crucified (Matt. 27:15–26; Mark 15:6–15; Luke 23:13–25; John 18:28–19:16)

Jesus' trial before the Sanhedrin was highly irregular. They held it at night, and Jesus was not given an opportunity to present witnesses in his defense. Even worse, the prosecution's witnesses told conflicting stories. Finally, they pronounced the death sentence immediately. Normally, a sentence of death required a day's wait before it was delivered.

Jesus Wears the Father's Crown (Matthew 27; Mark 15; Luke 23; John 19)

Crucifixion originated in the Persian practice of impaling enemies on single stakes and eventually made its way westward. The punishment was meant to maximize humiliation and deter other lawbreakers. It is recorded that Alexander the Great crucified two thousand Tyrians along the seashore after he had broken their siege.

The Roman author Seneca said it would be better to commit suicide than to be hung on a cross. Josephus called it "the most wretched of deaths." As a witness of the siege of Jerusalem in A.D. 70, he would have known the full horror of this tortuous means of execution. Reportedly, the Romans crucified so many Jews that the area immediately surrounding Jerusalem was stripped of trees. Cicero commented, "Let the very name of the cross be far away not only from the body of a Roman citizen, but even from his thoughts." In the Roman world, crucifixion was "the slaves' punishment" (*servile supplicium*), reserved for the lowest class and the outsider.

Jesus was whipped with a Roman scourge before his crucifixion.

The suffering of crucifixion was unimaginable. It balanced excruciating agony with maximum longevity, forcing the victim to spend as much time in conscious torment as possible. Crucified persons experienced the obvious pain of having nails pounded through their flesh and, in some cases, the bone. In addition, they faced exposure to the elements, insects, and in some cases, scavenging animals — with no means of self-defense. For most victims, the relief of death did not come any sooner than thirty-six hours. Sometimes, as a twisted form of mercy, the legs of the victim would be broken (or possibly severed) by a blow, hastening expiration through suffocation.

Jesus' suffering began long before he was nailed to the cross. From the moment of his arrest, he was beaten by soldiers of the Sanhedrin, his bound hands unable to deflect the blows. The scourging he received from the Roman soldiers frequently left some of their victims dead. Many testified that a person's gender and identity were hard to distinguish after such a beating. Jesus lost so much blood that carrying his cross became impossible for him.

In all of this, however, we must not forget that Jesus was not a helpless victim but a determined hero. In Gethsemane, he had made his intentions clear: "Not my will, but yours be done" (Luke 22:42). We must not forget that, ultimately, the hands of the Roman soldiers

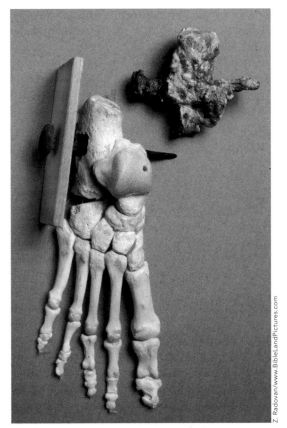

The heel bone of a crucified man is shown next to a model of a complete foot. The bone pierced by an iron nail was found in an ossuary in a Jerusalem tomb from the first century A.D.

were wielded by God himself, placing on Jesus the punishment our sins deserved. And in his death, Jesus secured his crown, having won for himself a people to call his own!

Discussion Questions

1. What does the cross tell us about God's view of sin? (Try to list and then discuss at least three things.)

2. "There are many paths to God." How does a thorough understanding of the cross help us respond to such a statement?

27

THE RESURRECTION

Plot Points

- Death is defeated by the resurrection: "Jesus is risen! He is risen indeed!"
- The gospel writers took great pains to demonstrate the historical reality of the resurrection.
- Jesus' resurrection is the beginning of the fulfillment of God's promised restoration of all things and the start of a new work of creation.

The Resurrection

Day	Event	Reference
Resurrection Sunday	The tomb visited by the women	Matt. 28:1; Mark 16:1
	The stone rolled away	Matt. 28:2–4
	The tomb found empty by the women	Matt. 28:5–8; Mark 16:2–8; Luke 24:1–8; John 20:1
	The tomb found empty by Peter and John	Luke 24:9–11; John 20:2–10
	Appearance to Mary Magdalene	Mark 16:9–11; John 20:11–18
	Appearance to the other women	Matt. 28:9–10
	Report of the soldiers to the Jewish authorities	Matt. 28:11–15
	Appearance to two disciples on the road to Emmaus	Mark 16:12–13; Luke 24:13–32
	The two disciples' reporting to the others	Luke 24:33–35
	Appearance to the ten assembled disciples	Luke 24:36–49; John 20:19–25
Sunday, one week later	Appearance to the Eleven assembled disciples	Mark 16:14; John 20:26–31; 1 Cor. 15:5
Sometime later	Appearance to seven disciples while fishing in Galilee	John 21:1–25
Still later	Appearance to the Eleven in Galilee, then to the 500	Matt. 28:16–20; Mark 16:15–19; 1 Cor. 15:6
Again still later	Appearance to James, Jesus' brother	1 Cor. 15:7
Forty days after resurrection	Appearance to the disciples in Jerusalem	Luke 24:44–53; Acts 1:3–8
	Jesus' ascension	Luke 24:50–53; Acts 1:9–12

Adapted from Robert L. Thomas, *Charts of the Gospels and the Life of Christ*, 97–98.

Cast of Characters

Chief priests. Asked Pilate to make Jesus' tomb secure and conspired with the guard to cover up the resurrection.

Cleopas. One of the two travelers on the Emmaus road who met the risen Christ; gave witness to the apostles of Jesus' resurrection; name means "renowned father."

James. One of Jesus' twelve apostles; witnessed Jesus' resurrection; while fishing with Peter, met the resurrected Jesus on the banks of Galilee.

Jesus. Born of a virgin; descendant of David and Adam; God in human form; the Son of God; the hero of *The Story*; defeated sin and death on the cross and in his resurrection.

John. One of Jesus' twelve apostles; the "disciple whom Jesus loved" who ran with Peter to witness the empty tomb; took care of Mary, mother of Jesus; author of the gospel that bears his name.

Joseph of Arimathea. Jewish man who donated his tomb for Jesus' body; bravely requested Jesus' body from Pilate; name means "may [God] add."

Mary. Mother of James. Present at the crucifixion; went early on the third day to anoint Jesus' body; discovered the empty tomb.

Mary Magdalene. Delivered from demons by Jesus; present at the crucifixion; went early on the third day to anoint Jesus' body; the first person on record to have encountered the risen Christ.

Nathanael. Also called Bartholomew; one of Jesus' twelve apostles; while fishing with Peter, met the resurrected Jesus on the banks of Galilee.

Nicodemus. A Pharisee who questioned Jesus early in his ministry; a disciple; defended him before the Sanhedrin; provided myrrh and aloes for anointing Jesus' body.

Peter. Raced with John to the empty tomb; jumped from a fishing boat to be with the risen Lord; personally commissioned to feed Jesus' sheep, the church; see previous chapters.

Pilate. See previous chapter.

Thomas. One of Jesus' twelve apostles; asked hard questions and looked for solid answers; sometimes lacked faith; refused to accept the testimony of his fellow apostles and disciples; insisted he would need to put his fingers in Jesus' wounds; quickly believed after seeing the resurrected Jesus; while fishing with Peter, again met the resurrected Jesus on the banks of Galilee.

Chapter Overview

As you reflect on this chapter, consider Paul's comments on the resurrection in 1 Corinthians 15:1 – 8, 11 – 26, 32:

Now, brothers and sisters, I want to remind you of the gospel I preached to you, which you received and on which you have taken your stand. By this gospel you are saved, if you hold firmly to the word I preached to you. Otherwise, you have believed in vain.

For what I received I passed on to you as of first importance: that Christ died for our sins according to the Scriptures, that he was buried, that he was raised on the third day according to the Scriptures, and that he appeared to Cephas, and then to the Twelve. After that, he appeared to more than five hundred of the brothers and sisters at the same time, most of whom are still living, though some have fallen asleep. Then he appeared to James, then to all the apostles, and last of all he appeared to me also, as to one abnormally born.... this is what we preach, and this is what you believed.

But if it is preached that Christ has been raised from the dead, how can some of you say that there is no resurrection of the dead?

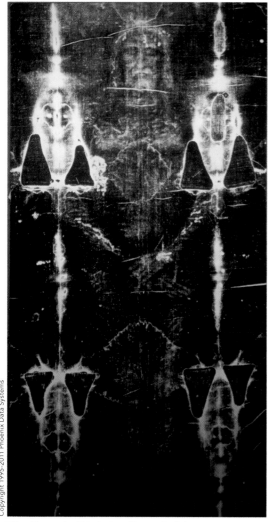

The Shroud of Turin is a linen cloth bearing the image of a man who appears to have been crucified. Some believed this to be the burial cloth of Jesus. However, radiocarbon dating tests done in 1988 showed the material dated to A.D. 1260–1390, which was centuries after Jesus' death.

If there is no resurrection of the dead, then not even Christ has been raised. And if Christ has not been raised, our preaching is useless and so is your faith. More than that, we are then found to be false witnesses about God, for we have testified about God that he raised Christ from the dead. But he did not raise him if in fact the dead are not raised. For if the dead are not raised, then Christ has not been raised either. And if Christ has not been raised, your faith is futile; you are still in your sins. Then those also who have fallen asleep in Christ are lost. If only for this life we have hope in Christ, we are to be pitied more than all others.

But Christ has indeed been raised from the dead, the firstfruits of those who have fallen asleep. For since death came through a human being, the resurrection of the dead comes also through a human being. For as in Adam all die, so in Christ all will be made alive. But in this order: Christ, the firstfruits; then, when he comes, those who belong to him. Then the end will come, when he hands over the kingdom to God the Father after he has destroyed all dominion, authority and power. For he must reign until he has put all his enemies under his feet. The last enemy to be destroyed is death.... If the dead are not raised, "Let us eat and drink, for tomorrow we die."

Section Commentary

Into the Tomb (Matthew 27; John 19)

The evangelists were careful to emphasize that Jesus was *really dead*. The Roman soldiers, skilled at determining the time of death by sight, also confirmed Jesus was dead by piercing his side with a spear, penetrating his heart. John emphasized in his gospel account that "he tells the truth" about Jesus' death, and he repeatedly uses the word "body" to emphasize that Jesus was dead: Joseph asked "for the body"; they took "the body"; they wrapped "the body" with spices; the Pharisees feared the disciples might "steal the body." Just as each one of us will die someday (unless the Lord first returns), Jesus experienced death and was buried in a tomb where his body lay for several days.

A tomb near Megiddo shows a rolling stone, similar to Jesus' tomb as described in the Bible.

Resurrection (Mark 16; John 20)

Just as they are careful to emphasize the actual death of Jesus, the gospel writers also present a strong set of proofs that Jesus actually rose from the dead. Here are a few:

1. *The tomb was empty.* The early Christians' claim that Jesus had risen could easily have been disproven. After all, Jesus had been a prominent figure, known throughout Galilee and in Jerusalem. The moment the disciples raised their voices, the religious leaders could have silenced them by simply pointing to the body lying in the tomb.

2. *The body was missing.* Of course, an empty tomb could have simply meant that the body was taken. But the gospel writers carefully describe details about the grave to emphasize that something unusual had happened. For instance,

John notes that Jesus' grave clothes were folded and laid on the table. The signs point not to a body stolen, but a body raised. It is difficult to believe that the disciples of Jesus would willingly face torture and death (as many did) for a body they had stolen themselves.

3. *He appeared to many people.* More than five hundred people directly encountered the risen Jesus, and not just once or twice. Jesus spent forty days teaching his followers. Since many of these witnesses were still alive at the time the Gospels were written, their accounts could easily have been verified.

4. *He changed many lives.* The Gospels are clear: when Jesus was arrested, his disciples fled for their lives. They abandoned their teacher and fled to safety. Clearly, there were no heroes in this group of followers. So why in the

world would these same disciples stand up — just a few months later — and risk their lives by publicly proclaiming a message they knew was a lie? Only fifty days following the resurrection, the same Peter who had been unwilling even to admit a passing acquaintance with Jesus stood up in the public square and preached boldly in Jesus' name.

Questions and Answers (Luke 24)

Two important themes are emphasized in the stories of the Emmaus road and Thomas's doubt. The first is that the Holy Spirit must open our eyes to accept and believe in Jesus Christ. In Romans 1:18 Paul declares that unbelievers "suppress the truth by their wickedness." In other words, their sin leads them to not believe what they know to be true. All the proofs in the world cannot *save* a person. The ultimate problem for each of us is not a lack of information, but that we are spiritually dead to God and need to be born anew through the work of the Holy Spirit.

Second, Jesus' words to Thomas — "blessed are those who have not seen and yet have believed" — are not an endorsement for "blind" faith. Thomas's problem was his lack of faith in God's Word. Jesus himself had explained to Thomas and the other disciples his coming death *and* resurrection. Knowing what Jesus had foretold, the other disciples' testimonies to Thomas should have caused him to remember, trust, and believe in Jesus' and Scripture's promise of the Messiah's resurrection. Instead, he doubted until he could physically touch and see evidence of the resurrection. Jesus blesses those who accept the promise of God's Word and trust the testimony of his appointed witnesses.

Restored and Commissioned
(Matthew 28; John 21)

Jesus' encounter with Peter should bring hope to us all. Although Peter had denied him several times, Jesus did not deny Peter. He restored him to service and gave him a mission. And like Peter, despite our failures and mistakes, we have also been called to serve and fulfill the mission of Jesus.

Discussion Questions

1. Why is it significant that the gospel authors emphasized that Jesus was really dead?

2. Paul said that if Jesus did not really rise, then we are most to be pitied. Why?

3. Woody Allen once said, "I don't want to achieve immortality through my work.... I want to achieve it through not dying." How does Allen's quote cut through our culture's sentimental way of handling death? How does Christ's resurrection address Allen's concern?

NEW BEGINNINGS

28

Plot Points

- Having given his disciples final instructions, Jesus ascends into heaven with a promise to return.
- At the Pentecost festival, the Holy Spirit falls on the disciples, unleashing powerful ministry of the gospel in words and in deeds of healing.
- The disciples are transformed from fearful cowards to fearless preachers in the face of the religious leaders' persecution.
- The death of Stephen, the first martyr, is a catalyst for the spread of the message and the growth of the church.
- The Gentiles are welcomed into the fellowship of the church and are no longer "unclean," excluded from membership in God's family.

The Early Church (A.D. 30–95)

Biblical	Secular
30 Coming of the Holy Spirit at Pentecost	36 Pilate dismissed by Rome
35 Paul converted to Christianity	37–41 Emperor Caligula
44 James martyred, Peter imprisoned	37–44 Herod Agrippa I
46–48 Paul's first missionary journey	41–54 Emperor Claudius
49/50 Jerusalem Council	49 Jews expelled from Rome
50–52 Paul's second missionary journey	54–68 Emperor Nero
53–57 Paul's third missionary journey	52–59 Felix as procurator
57–59 Paul's imprisonment in Caesarea	59–61 Festus as procurator
59–62 Paul's first imprisonment in Rome	64 Great fire in Rome; persecution of Christians
67/68 Paul's second imprisonment in Rome and execution	66 Jewish revolt; Jerusalem church scattered
90–95 John exiled on Patmos	69–79 Emperor Vespasian
95 Revelation written	70 Fall of Jerusalem
	73 Fall of Masada
	79–81 Emperor Titus
	81–96 Emperor Domitian; great persecution

Cast of Characters

Alexander. A member of the high priest's family; present at Peter and John's trial; name means "defender of man."

Ananias. A disciple from Damascus; called by Jesus to restore Paul's sight; helped instruct Paul; name means "protected by the Lord."

Annas. High priest who questioned Peter and John; also involved in the trial of Jesus; name means "grace."

Barnabas. Jewish Christian; helped oversee the church in Antioch; friend and companion of Paul on missionary journeys; name means "son of encouragement."

Blastus. Personal servant of Herod Agrippa I; name means "buds or brings forth."

Caiaphas. High priest who questioned Peter and John; antagonized the early believers; name means "depression."

Cornelius. A Roman centurion; from Caesarea; a God-fearer; as a result of Peter's visit, he and his whole family accepted the gospel and, like the Jewish believers at Pentecost, spoke in tongues; among the first of the Gentiles to be brought into the covenant community; name means "of a horn."

Gamaliel. Grandson of Rabbi Hillel; a Pharisee of importance; instructed Paul as a young man; advised moderation and tolerance in the Sanhedrin's approach to the early Christians.

James. Son of Zebedee; brother of John; apostle of Jesus Christ; put to death with the sword by King Herod.

Jesus. Risen Lord and Savior; God incarnate; spent forty days following his resurrection teaching his disciples.

John. Apostle of Jesus Christ; leader in the early church.

John. Member of the high priest's family; present at Peter and John's trial.

Judas. Man from Damascus; lived on Straight Street; housed Paul after he had been blinded.

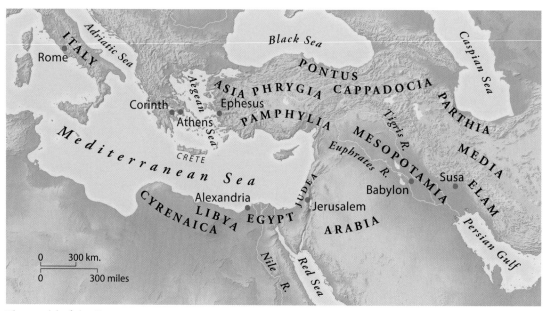

The world of the Pentecost.

Judas the Galilean. Led a failed rebellion; referenced by Gamaliel in his defense of the apostles before the Sanhedrin.

King Herod. Herod Agrippa I; grandson of Herod the Great; persecuted the early church to gain favor with the Jews.

Lame man. Unnamed man; healed by Peter and John on their way to the temple.

Mark. Also called John Mark; a relative of Barnabas; author of the gospel that bears his name.

Mary. Mother of Mark (John Mark); prayer meeting in her home visited by Peter after his miraculous escape from prison.

Paul. Originally called Saul ("demanded"); a highly educated Pharisee; a zealous man who initially opposed the Way of Jesus; radically converted when he encountered the risen Lord; planted churches throughout the first-century world; authored most of the New Testament; name means "small."

Peter. An apostle of Jesus; key leader in the early church; preached the great Pentecost sermon through which three thousand were baptized; helped open the door to Gentile inclusion in the church; put on trial and jailed by religious leaders for his confession of Jesus Christ.

Philip. Apostle of Jesus; after the persecution in Jerusalem that followed Stephen's murder, went to proclaim the gospel in a city in Samaria; did many signs in his ministry.

Rhoda. Servant in Mary's (mother of Mark) household; had a difficult time convincing other believers that the Lord had answered their prayers and freed Peter from prison; name means "rose."

Simon. A friend of Peter's; name means "hearing."

Stephen. The first Christian martyr; a Greek-speaking Jew; one of the seven entrusted with administration of relief funds in the Jerusalem church; a distinguished speaker filled with faith; forgave the Jewish leaders even as they stoned him to death; name means "crown."

Theophilus. Person to whom the gospel of Luke and Acts of the Apostles is addressed; means "God lover."

Theudas. Led a failed rebellion; referenced by Gamaliel in his defense of the apostles before the Sanhedrin; name means "gift of God."

Chapter Overview

The book of Acts is about the *activities* of the apostles. More specifically we could say it is about the spread of the gospel through the apostolic ministry. The book of Acts tells the story of how the gospel spread from a Jewish subculture into every culture!

It is interesting to consider why God chose someone like Paul to do the majority of this work. Paul, the Pharisee of Pharisees, was trained and schooled in the nuances of Jewish religious life. He seems an unlikely candidate to advocate bringing Gentiles — non-Jews — into full inclusion in the covenant community — without the mark of circumcision, without observing the law, and without adopting Jewish rituals. But God chose to use this "Jew of Jews" to expand his family to the nations of the world.

Of course, this transition did not happen solely through Paul's efforts. Although Paul is clearly the "missionary to the Gentiles" in Acts, he was not the one who initially opened that door. As we see, it all started with Peter.

Section Commentary

Final Lessons (Acts 1)

The New Testament relies heavily on the Old Testament — the Hebrew Scriptures. There are literally hundreds of instances when the New Testament authors, commenting on a gospel matter, turn to the Old Testament and quote a passage from the Law or the Prophets. One obvious reason for this is that these were men who had grown up learning the Hebrew Scriptures, and the Word of God was familiar to them. But another reason for the numerous references to the Old Testament can be traced directly to Jesus. Jesus spent forty days with his apostles after his resurrection from the dead, showing them how the Old Testament Scriptures were really all about him! The early church's understanding of Jesus and his significance came from more than careful reflection and study — they were taught the meaning of God's Word by Jesus himself.

Fire (Acts 2–5)

References to fire are found throughout the Old Testament: Moses and the burning bush;

According to tradition, the Upper Room was the location of Pentecost. However, this room was not even built until the twelfth century.

Israel at Mount Sinai; the pillar of fire by night that guided Israel through their travels; Elijah and the prophets of Baal; and chariots of fire. Fire was often a symbol of the Lord's presence. Deuteronomy 4:24 tells us, "The LORD your God is a consuming fire."

Fire once again appeared on the day of Pentecost. The Holy Spirit fell on all the believers gathered together. This time, however, he did not simply come upon them for a specific job, as he did the judges in the Old Testament. He filled them and remained with them, empowering them for the mission that Jesus had given to them, to be his witnesses to the nations. The people of God had now become God's holy temple, replacing the man-made temple of stones and bricks. The opening chapters of the book of Acts give us a picture of what it looks like when God comes to live with — and in — human beings.

Martyr and Missionaries (Acts 6–8)

The Greek word *marturos* has, through the centuries, been incorporated into two English words we commonly use. The first is easy to see: the word *martyr*. The second is somewhat less obvious: the word *witness*. Stephen was both of these as he stood before the Sanhedrin and fell before their stones. He was the first person to be killed for his confession of Jesus Christ.

Stephen's death opened a new period of persecution for the church in Jerusalem. But rather than stifling the spread of the gospel and the growth of God's people, it spurred them on in mission. Like wind blowing on the seeds of a dead dandelion, persecution spread the "seeds" of the gospel message outward to the world.

But Stephen's death also prompted another form of missionary zeal. Saul, a young, zealous

Scala/Art Resource, NY

The Martyrdom of Saint Stephen by Pietro di Miniato (1366–1450).

Pharisee, was inspired in his own mission—to destroy the early Christian church.

The Voice (Acts 9)

The conversion of Saul is, perhaps, one of the most significant events in history, second only to the death and resurrection of Jesus. God chose an unlikely person to accomplish unprecedented works for the kingdom. As he rode to Damascus, muttering threats and curses against the church, Saul encountered a light and a voice that changed everything! His zeal for God was transformed and redeemed.

Ananias heard this same voice instructing him to welcome Saul into his home, and over several days Saul's hatred of Christians was transformed into a love for Christ and his church. Saul became Paul, an apostle and leader of the early church and the author of many of the letters in the New Testament.

What God Made Clean (Acts 10)

Cornelius was evidently a "God-fearing man," a Gentile who worshiped at synagogue, seeking to know the God of Israel. He was attempting to live a righteous life, giving alms and supporting the work of God's kingdom as best he could. These things, of course, could not save him, but they were an indication of his openness and humility. It is no surprise that the Lord chose to work through this man to break down the walls that had previously existed between the Jews and the Gentiles. His entrance into the church began one of the greatest movements in history, the movement of the gospel into all nations.

The Hammer Falls (Acts 12)

When Herod saw that his execution of John the Baptist bought him favor with the Jewish leaders, he extended his persecution, eventually bringing the hammer down on the growing church. Little did he know that the hammer of God's judgment was about to fall on him. In addition to the biblical story of Herod's death, it was also recorded and described by an extrabiblical source. Jewish historian Flavius Josephus wrote:

> Now, when Agrippa had reigned three years over all Judaea, he went to the city of Caesarea …; and there he exhibited shows in honour of Claudius Caesar.… On the second day of the shows Agrippa put on a garment made wholly of silver … and came into the theatre at daybreak; at which time the silver of his garment being illumined by the early rays of the sun's beams upon it, glittered in a surprising manner, and was so resplendent as to inspire fear and trembling in those that looked intently upon him. And straightway his flatterers cried out … that "he was a god." … Upon this the king did neither rebuke them, nor reject their impious flattery. But soon afterwards he looked up, and saw an owl sitting on a certain rope over his head, and immediately understood that this bird was the messenger of ill tidings.… A severe pain also seized his belly, and began in a most violent manner.… And

The Conversion of St. Paul by Michelangelo Merisi da Carvaggio (1571 – 1610).

when he had been quite worn out by the pain in his belly for five days, he departed this life, being in the fifty-fourth year of his age. (Flavius Josephus, *The Works of Flavius Josephus*, trans. William Whiston, rev. A. R. Shilleto [London: George Bell and Sons, 1898], 19.7.2)

Discussion Questions

1. Compare the Peter we read about in the Gospels to the Peter we read about in the opening chapters of Acts. What are the chief similarities? What are the chief differences?

2. The early church struggled to unite very different peoples. What steps did it take for them to become a united body? What can we learn from their example?

PAUL'S MISSION

29

Plot Points

- The early church exhibited a vibrant prayer life and dependence on the Holy Spirit's guidance.
- The church spread by forming disciples, people who were capable of forming other disciples.
- The church spread through the Roman world like wildfire in a forest.

Paul's Missionary Journeys

Place	Date	Acts	Significant Events
First Missionary Journey			
Cyprus	47–48	13:1–12	Bar-Jesus blinded; proconsul Sergius Paulus converted; Saul called Paul
Perga in Pamphylia	48–49	13:13	John Mark returns home
Pisidian Antioch		13:14–52	Paul and Barnabas preach to Jews and Gentiles in synagogue; Jews stir up persecution against Paul and Barnabas and expel them from region
Iconium		14:1–5	Many Jews and Gentiles believe; unbelieving Jews cause division in city
Derbe		14:20–21	Many people get saved
Lystra, Iconium, Pisidian Antioch		14:21–23	Disciples strengthened and encouraged; elders appointed
Pamphylia		14:24–25	Travel to Pamphylia, Perga, and Attalia
Antioch		14:26–28	Report on gospel being accepted by Gentiles
Second Missionary Journey			
Antioch	49–51	15:36–40	Paul and Barnabas disagree over John Mark
Syria and Cilicia	50–52	15:41	Paul takes Silas with him
Derbe		16:1–3	Timothy joins Paul and Silas
Lystra, Iconium		16:1–5	Churches strengthened and growing
Phrygia, Galatia		16:6–7	Preaching throughout region

Place	Date	Acts	Significant Events
Troas	50–52 *cont.*	16:8–9	Paul receives vision to go to Macedonia
Philippi		16:10–40	Lydia converted; demon-possessed fortune-teller delivered; Paul and Silas jailed; jailer converted after earthquake
Thessalonica		17:1–9	Jews, Greek men and women believe; jealous Jews riot and mob Jason's house
Berea		17:10–14	Jews, Greek men and women believe; Jews from Thessalonica cause turmoil
Athens		17:15–34	Paul preaches about "Unknown God"; a few believe
Corinth	52	18:1–17	Crispus converted; Paul receives vision to stay; many Corinthians believe and are baptized; Paul meets Aquila and Priscilla; Sosthenes beaten
Ephesus		8:18–21	Paul asked to stay and preach; declines and leaves Aquila and Priscilla
Third Missionary Journey			
Antioch	52–56	18:23	Beginning of journey
Galatia and Phrygia	53–56	18:23	Disciples strengthened
Ephesus		18:24–19:41	Miracles performed; gospel spreads widely and grows in power; silversmiths riot
Macedonia and Greece		20:1–6	Jews plot to assassinate Paul
Troas		20:7–12	Eutychus falls from window; Paul brings him back to life
Miletus		20:13–38	Paul bids farewell to Ephesian elders
Journey back to Jerusalem		21:1–16	Agabus warns Paul of what will happen in Jerusalem
Jerusalem		21:17–26	Paul reports what God has done among the Gentiles

See H. Wayne House, *Chronological and Background Charts of the New Testament*, 124–25.

Cast of Characters

Alexander. Spoke for the Jews in the Ephesus riot.

Apollos. A Jew from Alexandria; influential teacher in the early church; knew Scripture well; learned from Aquila and Priscilla.

Aquila. Married to Priscilla; a Jewish Christian; capable of teaching others in the faith; friend and supporter of Paul.

Aristarchus. Christian from Thessalonica; traveled and spent time in jail with Paul; name means "best ruler."

Barnabas. Jewish Christian; helped oversee the church in Antioch; friend and companion of Paul on missionary journeys; name means "son of encouragement."

Chloe. Hosted a church in her home in Corinth; directly referenced by Paul in 1 Corinthians.

Claudius. Caesar, the emperor of Rome.

Crispus. Synagogue leader in Corinth; baptized by Paul after his conversion.

Demetrius. A silversmith in Ephesus; led a riot against Paul; name means "belonging to Demeter."

Elymas. Also called Bar-Jesus; Jewish sorcerer and false prophet; served Sergius Paulus, proconsul in Paphos; blinded by Paul.

Female slave. Unnamed character; afflicted with a demon and supposedly predicted the future; set free when Paul cast out the demon.

Gaius. Travel companion of Paul; seized in the Ephesus riot.

Gallio. Proconsul of Achaia; dismissed complaints against Paul lodged by Jewish leaders.

Jailer. Unnamed character; leader of a prison in which Paul was held; saved from suicide by Paul; he and his whole family converted.

Jason. Christian from Thessalonica; hosted Paul and Silas in his home; name means "healing."

John Mark. Nephew of Barnabas; part of Paul's first missionary journey; abandoned the journey at Asia Minor, leading to Paul's refusal to travel with him in the second missionary journey; eventually reconciled to Paul; wrote the gospel of Mark.

Lucias. A leader in the church at Antioch.

Luke. A physician; traveling companion of Paul; author of the gospel that bears his name and Acts of the Apostles; name means "luminous."

Lydia. Businesswoman from Thyatira; seller of dyed goods; converted through Paul's ministry; extended hospitality to Paul and Silas.

Manaen. A leader in the church at Antioch; "brought up with Herod," perhaps a person with political stature.

Paul. Originally called Saul ("demanded"); a highly educated Pharisee; a zealous man who initially opposed the Way of Jesus; radically converted when he encountered the risen Lord; planted churches throughout the first-century world; helped lead the church in Antioch; traveled with Barnabas, Silas, Timothy, and Luke, among others.

Priscilla. Married to Aquila; a Jewish Christian; capable of teaching others in the faith; friend and supporter of Paul.

Sceva. A Jewish chief priest.

Sceva's seven sons. Attempted to cast out demons in "the name of the Jesus whom Paul preaches"; embarrassed in the attempt.

Sergius Paulus. Roman proconsul in Cyprus impacted by Paul's ministry.

Silas. Traveled with Paul during most of his second missionary journey; prominent part of Jerusalem church; helped carry the decree of the Jerusalem Council (Acts 15); referred to as Silvanus in Paul and Peter's letters; name means "wood dweller."

Simeon. Called Niger; a leader in the church at Antioch.

Sosthenes. Leader in the synagogue at Corinth.

Timothy. Son of a heathen Greek father and a Jewish mother, Eunice; Paul's most well-known convert, disciple, traveling companion; gave significant leadership to the early church; name means "honoring God."

Titus Justus. A "worshiper of God"; provided a place for Paul to teach.

Tyrannus. Ephesian; had a lecture hall where Paul preached the gospel.

Chapter Overview

In this chapter we begin to see exactly why the Lord chose Paul to be his ambassador to the nations. Not only did Paul possess a brilliant theological mind, but he had an evangelist's zeal and a pastor's heart. Paul kept a near-frenetic pace, constantly traveling throughout the Mediterranean world. When he was not preaching or making tents, Paul was writing letters and forming disciples.

Below is a map showing each of Paul's three missionary journeys along with a short description of each mission.

Section Commentary

Paul's First Missionary Journey
(Acts 13 – 14)

The early church grew by balancing two critical practices. The first was a radical dependence on the Holy Spirit to lead them and guide them in mission. The decision of Paul to set out on his first missionary journey grew out of a concentrated season of prayer with several prophets and teachers in the church at Antioch.

The second practice of the early church was a strategic focus on key cultural centers. It is clear that Paul went to places where he could find potential leaders to carry the message forward. It was not an accident that he spread the message in the cities of the Roman world. Paul knew that these were the places where he would find the culture-shapers and communicators who could be discipled and sent out on mission. We also see that Paul had an intentional process that he followed in each city he visited. Paul started his work by seeking those who already exhibited faith in God, heading first to the synagogues.

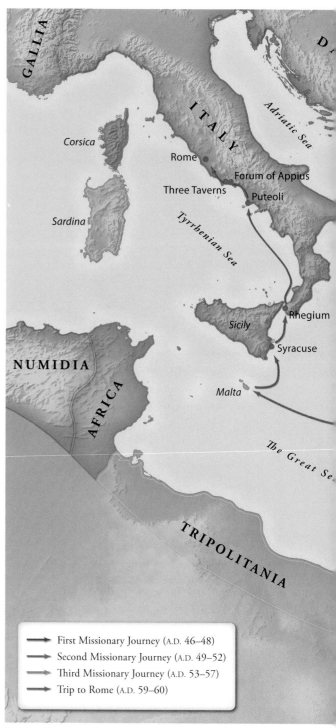

First Missionary Journey (A.D. 46–48)
Second Missionary Journey (A.D. 49–52)
Third Missionary Journey (A.D. 53–57)
Trip to Rome (A.D. 59–60)

Paul's missionary journeys.

GERMANIA

DACIA

MOESIA

MATIA

THRACE

Black Sea

MACEDONIA

Amphipolis
Philippi
Thessalonica
Neapolis
Berea
Appolonia?
Samothrace

BITHYNIA & PONTUS

GALATIA

EPIRUS

Mt. Olympus

Troas

MYSIA

ASIA

CAPPADOCIA

Ionian Sea

Delphi

Aegean Sea

Assos
Mitylene

Pergamum

COMMAGENE

Kios

Thyatira

LYCAONIA
Antioch (Pisidian)

Athens

LYDIA

Sardis

PISIDIA

Iconium

Euphrates R.

ACHAIA

Corinth

Smyrna
Ephesus

Philadelphia

PAMPHYLIA

Lystra

Derbe

CILICIA

Cenchrea

Samos

Laodicea

Tarsus

Issus

Patmos

Miletus

Colosse

SYRIA

Sparta

LYCIA

Attalia

Perga

Seleucia Pieria

Aleppo

Cos

Patara

Myra

Cyprus

Antioch
(Syrian)
(Antakya)

Cnidus

Rhodes

Perga

Salamis

Phoenix

Crete

Salmone

Paphos

ABILENE

Lasea

Fair Haven

PHOENICIA

Sidon

Damascus

The Great Sea

Tyre
Ptolemais

Caesarea Maritima

JUDEA

CYRENAICA

EGYPT

Jordan R.
Jerusalem

Salt Sea

ARABIA

Nile R.

0   200 km.
0   200 miles

Red Sea

Todd Bolen/www.BiblePlaces.com

A view of the excavations at Corinth, one of the major cities of Paul's missionary journeys.

Paul's Second Missionary Journey
(Acts 16 – 18; 1 Thessalonians 1 – 5)

Paul's second missionary journey is notable for three key reasons. First, the journey began with a tragic separation from his friend Barnabas over a dispute. Second, Paul pushed farther toward Rome. Leaving the cities of Asia Minor, Paul headed into Macedonia and Greece, visiting some of the most influential urban centers of his day. Finally, on this mission trip, Paul met a young man named Timothy and invited him to join him, assisting him in his missionary work. Timothy became like a son to Paul and was himself a significant leader in the early church.

Paul's Third Missionary Journey
(Acts 18 – 20; Romans 1, 2 – 6, 8, 12, 15; 1 Corinthians 1, 2, 5 – 6, 10, 12 – 13, 15 – 16; Galatians 1, 3, 5 – 6)

Luke's narrative compresses large trips covering hundreds of miles of travel into just a few words. But even so, we can grasp the heart of this third missionary journey: to visit and build up churches. Paul's strategy was focused on building leaders who could build leaders. With pastoral sensitivity, he spent time nurturing key disciples and raising up men and women who would carry on his work of discipleship, long after he was gone.

Discussion Questions

1. How would you describe the balance between being "led by the Spirit" and being "led by good sense" in Paul's ministry?

2. How was Paul's ministry similar to the ministry of Jesus? In what ways are they different? What accounts for the differences?

The Library of Celsus at Ephesus, a city Paul visited on his second and third missionary journeys.

30 PAUL'S FINAL DAYS

Plot Points

- Jesus told his followers that they, like him, would be hated; Paul's story proves that this was true for his followers in the early church.
- Paul's ministry was lived out in the context of relationships and discipleship.
- Paul never wasted a moment. Whether writing letters or witnessing to Roman soldiers, he spent his entire life sharing the gospel and caring for the young, growing churches he had planted.

Paul's Letters

Book	Time of Writing	Place of Writing	Theme
Galatians	49, after 1st missionary journey	Antioch in Syria (?)	Justification by faith
1 Thessalonians	50–51, during 2nd missionary journey	Corinth	Second Coming described
2 Thessalonians	50–51, during 2nd missionary journey	Corinth	Second Coming clarified
1 Corinthians	54, during 3rd missionary journey	Ephesus	Aspects of Christian conduct
2 Corinthians	55, during 3rd missionary journey	Macedonia	Portrayal of Christian ministry
Romans	55, during 3rd missionary journey	Corinth	Doctrine of salvation
Philemon	60	Rome	Favor requested of a friend
Colossians	60	Rome	Christ completes the believer
Ephesians	60	Rome	Believer's position in Christ
Philippians	61	Rome	Believer's attitude in Christ
1 Timothy	62	Macedonia	Conduct for church described
Titus	62	Nicopolis	Importance of sound doctrine and good works
2 Timothy	63	Rome	Final charge to a disciple

H. Wayne House, *Chronological and Background Charts of the New Testament*, 16–17, 21.

Cast of Characters

Agabus. Prophet from Jerusalem; predicted a famine; predicted Paul would be arrested if he returned to Jerusalem; name means "locust."

Ananias. High priest; oversaw Paul's trial before the Sanhedrin; ordered an attendant to strike Paul; aware of and colluded with the plot to kill Paul; name means "protected by the Lord."

Aristarchus. Christian from Thessalonica; traveled and spent time in jail with Paul; name means "best ruler."

Carpus. Mentioned in Paul's second letter to Timothy.

Claudius Lysias. Roman commander who protected Paul from an assassination attempt.

Crescens. A friend to Paul during his imprisonment in Rome.

Demas. A friend of Paul's who later deserted him.

Felix. Roman governor of Judea; heard Paul's case in Caesarea; imprisoned him for two years; name means "happy."

Festus. Followed Felix as governor of Judea; honored Paul's appeal to Caesar.

Herod Agrippa II. Ruled in Galilee; provided advice from Festus regarding Paul.

Julius. Centurion; member of the imperial regiment; had custody of Paul and other prisoners in the journey to Rome; showed Paul kindness.

Luke. A physician; traveling companion of Paul; author of the gospel that bears his name and Acts of the Apostles; name means "luminous."

Mark. Mentioned by Paul in his second letter to Timothy; as a young man, had abandoned a trip with Paul; later in life, viewed favorably by Paul; wrote the gospel that bears his name.

Philip. One of the seven appointed to administer relief funds; an evangelist whose four unmarried daughters prophesied; hosted Paul on his journey back to Jerusalem.

Publius. Chief official on Malta; his father healed by Paul.

Timothy. Son of a heathen Greek father and a Jewish mother, Eunice; Paul's most well-known convert, disciple, traveling companion; gave significant leadership to the early church; name means "honoring God."

Titus. Discipled by Paul; received a personal letter from Paul, informing his leadership in the early church.

Trophimus. An Ephesian; traveled with Paul.

Tychicus. Travel companion for Paul; also entrusted with delivering messages for Paul.

Chapter Overview

As we have already noted, Paul kept up a tiring schedule, constantly traveling. He was, without a doubt, a man of action. Yet Paul also had an incredible focus on building relationships. One of the clearest indicators of this comes when we read the end of each of his letters. In most of them, we find an extensive list of people he is praying for and thinking about. Each name in the letters represents a personal relationship Paul has built, and it is through these kinds of relationships — and the love and encouragement so evident in his letters — that disciples are made.

Section Commentary

The Journey Continues (Acts 20 – 21)

Paul had sensed God's call to head to Jerusalem. Part of the reason for this trip was to deliver the offering he had collected from the Gentile churches in Greece and Asia Minor. In several passages of Scripture (Romans 15:25 – 26; 1 Corinthians 16:1 – 4; and 2 Corinthians 8:10 – 15), Paul refers to this offering, a collection that he had taken more than one year to gather. Paul saw this trip to Jerusalem as a final seal on the work the Holy Spirit had been doing to unite Jews and Gentiles in the early church. The generosity of the Gentile churches and their gifts for the Jewish believers in Jerusalem were evidence of their love for one another and their unity in Christ, despite their racial, cultural, and socioeconomic differences.

Into the Fire (Acts 21 – 23)

Paul arrived in Jerusalem sometime around June, in the year A.D. 58. Sadly, though Jerusalem had once been his home, Paul was now an unwelcome guest because of his consistent preaching in the name of a condemned and executed "disturber of the peace." To add insult to injury, Paul had also committed a terrible

An aerial view of Rome—a large city even in the time of Paul, with a population of more than 1 million.

crime: he had reached out to the *Gentiles*! Just as they had with Jesus, the religious leaders plotted to kill Paul.

Shipwrecked (Acts 27 – 28)

Travel in the ancient world was fraught with peril. Although the *pax Romana* ("peace of Rome") extended to the roadways, there was nothing that could control the chaotic and stormy seas. In these passages, Luke's literary brilliance shines through.

More importantly, we continue to see that even though Paul was traveling from city to city, he was always involved in the work of ministry. These were not vacations or simple visits with friends; Paul was intentionally focused on preaching the good news about Jesus wherever he went. Even as he traveled to Rome for his trial, Paul demonstrated the heart of a pastor, caring for the spiritual needs of his fellow travellers.

The Mamertine Prison is generally accepted as the place where Paul and Peter were imprisoned in Rome.

A Letter (Ephesians 1 – 6; 2 Timothy 1 – 4)

Paul led a full life — walking dusty roads, riding on donkeys, running from mobs, and rolling on the open sea — yet he still found time in his free moments to pen letters to his friends and to the churches he had planted. Paul rarely wasted a moment of time, and his example should challenge us today to make the most of our own time and opportunities. We live in a world of incredible opportunities to communicate and share the message of Christ, but it is a world that also includes the potential of wasting our time on meaningless distractions. Paul's example and his constant care for the churches under his care should challenge us to make the most of the days we have been given.

Discussion Questions

1. Paul willingly put himself in danger for the sake of the gospel. What provided him with the courage to do this?

2. At several points in the story we see Paul share his testimony. How would you summarize his message? Describe how God may have used your testimony as a witness for him.

31 THE END OF TIME

Plot Points

- God is on the throne of eternity, no matter what we experience on this earth.
- Jesus Christ, the Lamb who was slain, stands forever before the throne of God, a constant witness to the security of our salvation.
- One day soon, all things will be made new and God will live with humanity on earth.

The Cities of the Seven Churches of Revelation

City	Description
Ephesus	Revelation 2:1–7
	Population 200,000–500,000; important trade port in Asia Minor; a "free city" in Roman Empire, received Roman citizenship; 25,000-seat theater; worshiped Artemis, whose priestesses were cult prostitutes; also worshiped Emperor Domitian
Smyrna	Revelation 2:8–11
	Population 200,000; harbor town; wealthy community of academics; one street made of gold and bounded by two temples
Pergamum	Revelation 2:12–17
	Made parchment; second-largest library in empire; location of the Asclepion, a health resort; famous altar to Zeus; three temples dedicated to emperor worship
Thyatira	Revelation 2:18–29
	Dominated by trade guilds; intersected an imperial post road
Sardis	Revelation 3:1–6
	A fortress city; wealthy; close to a fertile river basin; rebuilt by Tiberius after being destroyed by earthquake in A.D. 17
Philadelphia	Revelation 3:7–13
	A fortress city; intersected imperial post road; Hellenistic education center; rebuilt by Tiberius after being destroyed by earthquake in A.D. 17
Laodicea	Revelation 3:14–22
	Famous for producing black wool; banking center; medical school; suffered two earthquakes and rebuilt once without imperial aid

Cast of Characters

Four living creatures. Surrounded the throne of God, each with a different appearance — one like a lion, the second like an ox, the third with a face like a man, the fourth like a flying eagle — each one covered with eyes and with six wings; perhaps the cherubim of Genesis 3:24 and Ezekiel 1:10; 10:14; more than their appearance, important to note their function: to perpetually sing the song of the redeemed.

Jesus. Lord God; Son of Man; First and Last; Living One; Alpha and Omega; risen Lord; Lion of Judah; Lamb that was slain; Jesus appears at the center of all things as the focus of all worship.

John. The one who records the vision.

The King on the throne. God Almighty.

Twenty-four elders. Clothed in white; holding crowns; may represent the glorified church, uniting the twelve Old Testament tribes and the twelve New Testament apostles; more important than precisely identifying is grasping that these twenty-four dignitaries fall down before the throne and give perpetual worship to the Lamb.

Chapter Overview

The book of Revelation is often reduced to a strange blend between a complex crossword puzzle and a tricked-out tarot card. Interpreters become so focused on the things in Rev-elation that are not clear that they fail to high-light and celebrate the things that are *very* clear. And there are many clear, inspiring, stunning, and worship-inducing truths in the book of Revelation.

John's vision accomplishes something more than simply showing us the *future*. It shows us the *center*. It shows us that at the heart of every-thing, God reigns. It shows us that the God who reigns on a throne, high and holy, is also the Lord who sent his one and only Son to die on a cross and rescue sinners. The Lamb who was slain is now alive forevermore. For all eternity, we will see, savor, and celebrate the goodness and glory of the God who saves. This is how God wants to be known and revealed. And this is a vision that the church needs to remember — especially in the midst of persecution and suffering.

The story concludes with all that has been broken, restored. The lost have been found. Evil has been defeated. And the world is even

The Seven Churches of Revelation.

better than we could ever have imagined. For in the end, we learn that God does not simply re-create a beautiful world that has been marred and stained by human sin. The story of our redemption, healing, and the new work of creation through Jesus Christ shows us something deeper about God. In response to our sin and rebellion, God is both just and gracious. In his righteous judgment against sin, he has graciously made a way for his people to behold him, know him, and love him. That is what we were made to do, and it is the hope of our future: to live with God forever in a world renewed and freed from the curse of sin.

Section Commentary

The Risen Christ (Revelation 1)

In his first coming, Jesus' appearance was unremarkable. He suffered the insults of the religious leaders. He did not make the demands of a king. He came to serve, not to be served. He came to give his life as a ransom for many. The risen Lord Jesus is presented in this passage as a majestic, awe-inspiring figure. His glory shines like burnished bronze and resounds like rushing waters. Even so, John, the beloved disciple, recognized his Master's voice when he said, "Do not be afraid."

An aerial view of Patmos, where John received his Revelation.

The Bible speaks of Jesus "coming with the clouds" (Rev. 1:7) when he returns.

To the Churches (Revelation 2–3)

The churches Jesus addresses were in various states of spiritual health. Two were well-commended: Smyrna and Philadelphia. Two were harshly rebuked: Sardis and Laodicea. Three were a mixed bag: Ephesus, Pergamum, and Thyatira. It is interesting to note that the two "good" churches were composed of people on the lower rung of society, people persecuted for their faith. The two "bad" churches were groups that "had it all" according to worldly standards. Their members were well off and comfortable. Ephesus had good teaching but had forsaken their first love. Pergamum was fighting against the forces of heresy. Thyatira was in danger because they tolerated "Jezebel." Jesus has a word for our churches today as well. Will we be a church like those at Smyrna, or have we compromised our faith and become a Sardis or a Laodicea?

The Center of It All (Revelation 4)

Our world offers us many things on which to center our lives — sports, hobbies, social activism, politics, entertainment, art. Just dipping a toe into the subcultures that surround each of these pursuits will teach us something: each one of us can consume our imagination, attention, and passion. John presents us a picture of the *only* all-consuming center: the throne of God. This vision has the power to keep our hearts steady when we are tempted to fear or compromise our faith.

The Lion Is the Lamb (Revelation 5)

If heaven has tympanic drums, they would surely be rumbling as the angel declared, "See, the Lion of the tribe of Judah" (v. 5). Perhaps John blinked twice, though, when that Lion appeared in the form of a Lamb. The meaning of this unexpected image is simple: redemption is the ultimate revelation of God's kingdom rule. The Lamb that was slain is the Lion who rules. By his suffering, Jesus has secured redemption for God's people and is the only person qualified to rule God's kingdom.

The Warrior-King (Revelation 19)

Our world does not want to hear it, but one day, the world as we know it will end. The end of the world will not be the deep freeze of universal entropy, nor will it be a mass extinction as the planet is destroyed. The world will end when the King of Kings and Lord of Lords returns in judgment to establish once and for all God's visible, kingdom rule. On that day the one who was rejected by his own people will be revealed in his true glory, and every knee will bow and tongue confess, "Jesus Christ is Lord!"

The Judgment Throne
(Revelation 20)

Scripture is clear: each person will one day stand before God. Every single person will one day account for the life he or she lived. Every single action, thought, and motive will be laid before the Judge. Our only hope in that day will be the mercy of the cross. In Noah's day the ark was the place of safety and salvation from judgment. On that final day, faith in Jesus Christ and his sacrifice on our behalf will be our refuge from the wrath of a holy God.

Eden Again but Better
(Revelation 21 – 22)

We cannot imagine what the new heavens and new earth will be like. But we know this: they will be even better than what we can imagine. The restoration of all things is more than a "reset" button returning us to the garden of Eden. Humanity's long history was not an accident or mistake. The reality of sin and suffering in this world was not a detour from God's eternal plan. From the beginning God knew that we could only grasp his glory if we came to know him and love him as the God who saves. Eden was good. But the new heavens and new earth will be better, because we will see him for who *he* is — the God of our salvation.

Live for Then Right Now
(Revelation 22)

The story of God's salvation closes with a simple message: live today as if this story is real. If all of history will one day end in final judgment, then live with the awareness that you will be asked to account for the choices and decisions you make in this life. Since all of creation will one day be redeemed, live today as a minister of reconciliation, a representative of God to the world. And since every soul you encounter will one day stand before God's throne, be sure to hold out their only hope: Jesus. He is, after all, the hero of this story.

Discussion Questions

1. What are some ways people "miss it" when it comes to Revelation?

2. As you read through the letters to the churches in Asia Minor, what themes emerged as especially relevant to the American church?

RESOURCES
FOR FURTHER STUDY

If you dip your toe into the waters of biblical studies, you will find the pool is deep and the currents quick. Here are some helpful, practical, and challenging resources to further your study of the story of Scripture:

Zondervan has published an indispensable collection in its ZondervanCharts series. These resources are an excellent place to turn if you want to see how historical, thematic, theological, geographical, and/or archaeological data fit together. I referred to the following three books in the series:

House, H. Wayne. *Chronological and Background Charts of the New Testament.*

Thomas, Robert L. *Chronological and Background Charts of the Gospels and the Life of Christ.*

Walton, John H. *Chronological and Background Charts of the Old Testament.*

The Zondervan Illustrated Bible Background Commentary series (ZIBBC), Clinton E. Arnold, gen. ed., covers both the Old and New Testaments and provides an excellent combination of biblical commentary and visual resources. As the name suggests, each commentary is rich with illustrations and archaeological information. At the same time, these handy commentaries retain insightful commentary on the text itself.

Halley's Bible Handbook is an excellent, single-volume resource providing insight into every book in the Bible. Each page of the *Handbook* reflects the wisdom of a seasoned teacher.

The New Moody Atlas of the Bible is a wonderful combination of essays and maps. Each map is rich with detail yet does not demand a magnifying glass for practical use!

Finally, *The Baker Encyclopedia of Bible People*, Mark Water, ed., has biblical characters organized thematically in addition to an alphabetical index. Each character is given a brief description and verse references.